WHEN KIDS GO TO COLLEGE

A PARENT'S GUIDE TO CHANGING RELATIONSHIPS

Barbara M. Newman
& Philip R. Newman

WHEN
KIDS
GO TO
COLLEGE

A PARENT'S GUIDE TO CHANGING RELATIONSHIPS

OHIO STATE UNIVERSITY PRESS

COLUMBUS

Copyright © 1992 by the Ohio State University Press.
All rights reserved.

Library of Congress Cataloging-in-Publication Data

Newman, Barbara M.
When kids go to college : a parent's guide to changing
relationships / Barbara M. Newman and Philip R. Newman.
p. cm.
Includes bibliographical references.
ISBN 0-8142-0561-5 (alk. paper).
ISBN 0-8142-0562-3 (alk. paper : pbk.)
1. College students—United States—Psychology.
2. Parenting—United States. 3. Parent and child—
United States. I. Newman, Philip R. II. Title.
LA229.N43 1992
378.1'98—dc20   91-21700
                                                       CIP

Text and jacket design by Jim Brisson.
Type set in California, Avant Garde, and Bodoni by
Connell-Zeko Type & Graphics, Kansas City, MO.

The paper in this book meets the guidelines for permanence
and durability of the Committee on Production Guidelines for
Book Longevity of the Council on Library Resources. ∞

Printed in the U.S.A.

9 8 7 6 5 4 3 2

CONTENTS

PREFACE

When our oldest son, Sam, started college, we spent long hours talking together, trying to sort out our feelings and to make the best judgments we could about what was happening for our son and for us. We had to pay attention to the feelings of our younger children, who had reactions of their own to their brother's departure, as well as to Sam's reactions and to our own. As we talked, we discovered that many of the changes we were experiencing were changes in us and in our family as well as in him.

For many families, sending a child to college is a pragmatic move that serves as an investment to assure the child a secure, financially rewarding future. The emphasis on career goals and occupational preparation may overshadow the intellectual, social, and emotional growth that also occurs during these years. Students and parents may be bewildered as they discover that much more takes place during four or five years at college than meeting educational requirements and selecting a career.

Colleges have a wide variety of resources to meet students' needs and to help students cope with the challenges they confront. But parents are left pretty much empty-handed. We are greeted courteously, shown around the campus, encouraged to keep in touch, and sent periodic newsletters and reminders about upcoming campus events. Of course, we get the bills. But for the most part we are on our own as far as how we manage this major change in our family, how we understand what is happening for our college student, and how we understand our own feelings as the nature of our relationship with this child is transformed.

This book is written for parents of college students. We hope it will provide new ideas about your own development as well as your child's during this important period of family life.

Students make choices during their college years that form the core of their adult life-style. They set a course for adulthood that starts them on a path of commitments to actions, relationships, and goals. It takes the following ten or fifteen years for the consequences of their decisions to unfold. Their choices do not set permanent, unchangeable directions. New opportunities for change and growth occur throughout life. With contemporary adult life so filled with options—for work, marriage, parenting, and leisure activities—it is more essential now than ever before that young people make the best possible use of their college years.

One of the difficulties in discussing this period is highlighted by trying to select a term to use to refer to people who are attending college. In one sense, they are children. No matter how old they get, they are always children in a parent's eyes. Yet they bristle at being called children.

From another point of view, they are adolescents. They have just worked hard to master the intellectual, social, and emotional demands of the high school years. They have not taken on many of the roles and responsibilities that would give them adult status. Yet college students see themselves as distinct from the teenagers of the high school world. They do not like to be called adolescents.

In still another sense, they are young adults. They can vote, serve in the military, drive cars, establish credit, hold a steady job, and marry without their parents' consent. In their own eyes, they are much more a part of the adult world than the world of childhood. They prefer to be called young adults.

Yet parents, teachers, and others who work with college students realize that these young adults are in a period of rapid transformation and personal discovery. One of the reasons that working with college students can be so rewarding is exactly because of this sense of transition. The staff at your child's college, the advisors, the faculty, and the counselors take great satisfaction in knowing that they can make a significant difference in students' lives.

More happens in college than just the intellectual work involved in completing courses, selecting a major, and graduating. Students gain a very powerful psychological sense of themselves as independent and interdependent individuals who are ready to face the world on their own and who are ready to make commitments to people, values, and careers when the appropriate time arrives. Out of the tension created by the student's needs and desires and the pressures of social situations, a personal identity is formed.

Forming a personal identity is a very complex psychological process involving personal questioning, reflection, and self-examination. It leads to an understanding of one's strengths, weaknesses, and potentials, to the development of personal values, career directions, life-style preferences, and to a sense of oneself as a man or a woman. Young people begin to realize that commitments are necessary in order to achieve satisfaction in life. By the end of college, most students have the capacity to make the commitments to hard work and social relations that will help them achieve the kind of life they hope to create.

Personal identity and commitments are not necessarily the issues that parents and students consider when they think about college. However, they are among those that will surface. Identity formation pervades a student's thoughts and experiences. It is an integrative process that puts the finishing touches on an individual's ability to stand alone and with others—to take creative control of his or her own life and to make creative, harmonious contributions to the lives of others.

If parents understand more fully what is about to happen to their children, and how it affects them as well, they will be more effective in their roles as advocates and advisors. We offer our observations in the sincere hope that they will enrich your relationship with your children during the coming years when the dreams of a lifetime are taking shape.

The content of this book is drawn from a variety of sources. We have written several textbooks on human development, including books on adolescent development. The research literature that provides the basis for the observations in this book is reviewed more systematically in those texts. You will find a bibliography of texts and other source materials at the end of the book. We have suggested additional reading at the end of most chapters as well.

In past summers, Barbara had the privilege of speaking to parent groups during freshman orientation at The Ohio State University about the psychological tasks of development for students during the college years. Those lectures and the comments and questions parents raised during the discussion helped shape the content of this book. Recalling our own college years, working in colleges and universities for the past twenty-five years, experiencing our son's departure to college, and listening to the concerns of friends who are parents of college students have all influenced our thinking and the selection of topics for this book.

Chapter 1 introduces the dynamics of the changing parent-child relationship during the college years. Chapter 2 describes how the struggles and successes of the college years lead to the sense of one's self as an independent individual with personal resources who can grapple with the challenges of adulthood. This is called individual identity. Chapter 3 discusses the development of mature, independent values that occurs in college and how students' constant questioning of values helps our culture continuously review its own values. Chapter 4 presents the idea that each college and university has its own unique educational culture and discusses how to understand the impact of certain elements, such as living arrangements, on the quality of college life. Chapter 5 examines the importance of friendship and loneliness as they influence the student's development. Chapter 6 discusses the major role gender plays in giving students a sense of who they are. Romance and its impact on student development are covered in this chapter. Chapter 7 examines the process through which the college student gains a sense of self as a worker who can make important contributions and who can use work to establish an independent life. Selecting a major and a career are covered in this chapter. Chapter 8 presents some of the personal and social problems students may encounter and offers advice on how to help them deal with these problems.

The world of colleges and universities creates a culture with an organization all its own. Following is a list of titles and terms that are often used in discussing college life. Our definitions clarify these terms so that you can better negotiate the institutional bureaucracy and understand what your child is telling you about college.

TITLES AND TERMS

Entering the world of colleges and universities is quite similar to a journey to the Land of Oz. You will encounter new titles and terms as well as familiar terms that refer to something other than what you had expected. What is more, although colleges and universities share many common characteristics, each one has its own distinctive features. This list provides you with definitions of some common titles and terms used in American colleges and universities. You may want to pursue more specific meanings as they apply to the colleges or universities where your children are enrolled.

The list is presented first in alphabetical order, with the page numbers indicated, so you can quickly find a term that is of interest. The titles and terms are defined within ten general groupings so you can read about the related terms under one section. The groupings are College/University, Degrees, Administration, Faculty, Student Conduct, Honors/Placement, Courses, Financial Aid, Student Support Services, and Student Life.

COLLEGE / UNIVERSITY

College   An institution of higher learning (in the United States this means after high school) leading to a bachelor's degree. Colleges usually offer a variety of subjects leading to the degree. Colleges are usually divided into academic departments, such as psychology and physics. At universities the term *college* refers to one of a number of large academic units, each with a specific focus of study, such as the College of Mathematical and Physical Sciences or the College of Business. The academic departments are grouped within colleges.

Community College

An institution of higher learning that offers two years of general education courses that may be applied toward a bachelor's degree at a college or university, plus other technical and professional coursework. Community colleges are often non-residential (students commute to the campus from their homes). Students completing a program of study at a community college may be eligible for an associate's degree, certain types of technical certification, or both.

University

An institution of higher learning made up of an undergraduate division leading to the bachelor's degree, and graduate and professional divisions that confer master's degrees, doctorates, and professional degrees such as doctor of medicine, doctor of laws, and doctor of veterinary medicine.

Liberal Arts

The fields of study at a college or university that are intended to promote broad, intellectual capacities of judgment, reasoning, analysis, and critical thinking as compared to those programs of study intended to prepare students for specific professions. The liberal arts usually include the fields of philosophy, literature, history, languages, and the physical, natural, and social sciences. These fields may be contrasted to the professional areas, such as nursing, business, education, home economics, engineering, or agriculture. Some colleges are referred to as liberal arts colleges. This means that they emphasize the study of the disciplines mentioned above rather than the professional areas. When professional programs of study are offered at a university, they usually require students to enroll in a substantial number of courses from the liberal arts.

DEGREES

Bachelor's Degree   The first degree conferred by a college or university following completion of the undergraduate program. Many universities confer both the bachelor of arts (BA) and the bachelor of science (BS) degrees. These two degrees can often be distinguished by differences in the science, mathematics, research, and technical focus of the program of study. However, students at one college may receive the bachelor of arts degree whereas students at another college may receive the bachelor of science degree for study in the same basic field. Although many colleges design a curriculum that will lead to a bachelor's degree in four years, most universities find that students take an average of five years to complete the degree.

Master's Degree   The first degree after the bachelor's degree in the liberal arts. A master's degree usually requires one and a half to two years. Most fields within the liberal arts and many professional fields offer the master's degree. The most commonly earned master's degrees are the master of arts (MA) and the master of science (MS). Earning the master's degree usually involves completion of graduate-level course work and the preparation of a master's thesis or independent scholarly project. In some fields, like art, dance, and music, the MFA or master of fine arts is the most advanced degree possible. In other fields, such as business and education, the master's degree can be an important credential for occupational advancement. In still other fields, such as philosophy or chemistry, the master's degree is generally viewed as the first step on the way to the completion of the Ph.D.

Doctoral Degree

The doctoral degree, or Ph.D. (doctor of philosophy) is the highest academic degree. It is offered in most fields of the liberal arts as well as in many professional areas. The doctoral degree requires a combination of graduate course work; research experience; and the preparation of a dissertation, a major scholarly work that makes an original contribution to the discipline. Students may be enrolled for five to seven years, or longer if they stop from time to time, in order to complete the Ph.D. Most colleges and universities require their regular faculty members who teach at the undergraduate or the graduate levels to have completed the Ph.D.

ADMINISTRATION

President

The senior administrative officer at most colleges and universities is called the president. The president has responsibility for administering or managing all aspects of the institution, including the academic programs and faculty, physical facilities, personnel and hiring procedures, budget, programs directed toward student development, athletics, fund raising, relationships with the community, relationships with government agencies, and relationships with the alumni. Sometimes, when a college or university is part of a statewide system, the head of one university within the system is called the chancellor of that university and the head of the entire system is called the president. Sometimes the head of the statewide system is called the chancellor, and the head of each institution is called a president.

Provost   The provost is the senior administrator responsible for all the academic programs, colleges within a university, policies regarding enrollment and degree completion, and the promotion and tenure of the faculty. Sometimes the provost is called the vice president for academic affairs. Some colleges have a person with the title dean of the faculty who has these responsibilities.

Dean   Dean is a title used to designate the senior administrator of a college within a university as the dean of the College of Engineering, or the dean of the College of Arts and Sciences. The dean is like a president of his or her college. This person is responsible for the direction and quality of all the academic programs within the college; the direction of research in the college; faculty recruitment; the student support services, such as advising, tutoring, and career placement; relationships with alumni; and fund raising. Some decisions made by the dean are subject to a university-wide review, especially budgetary planning, changes in the academic program requirements or initiation of new programs, and recommendations for promotion and tenure of the faculty.

At many colleges, the title of dean is given to administrators who have major responsibility for college-wide functions, such as the dean of students or the dean of faculty.

Department Chairperson

The department chairperson is the administrative head of an academic department. In most colleges, the department chairperson reports to the dean of faculty; in most universities, the department chairperson reports to the dean of the college in which the department is located. Department chairs, sometimes referred to as department heads, are critical administrators in any college or university. They are faculty members who assume a leadership role for one or more terms. They are often active faculty members who have teaching, research, and professional responsibilities and who are directly in charge of the direction and quality of programs in their academic disciplines. They work with faculty in the department to provide the best possible academic programs for students, to resolve problems, and to encourage the continued professional growth of the faculty members.

Academic Department

These are the basic organizational units of any college or university. Departments are to colleges as families are to society. The departments focus on a subject matter, such as English, chemistry, sociology, or botany, or on some multidisciplinary area of study such as family relations or Hispanic studies. The number and types of departments differ widely from college to college. To learn about the types of departments and the kinds of courses they offer, a student must refer to the college catalog (sometimes referred to as the course bulletin), where all the departments and their course offerings are listed.

FACULTY

Faculty   The term *faculty* can refer to the entire group of individuals in a college or university, to the members of a department, such as the faculty of the department of history, or to an individual person as a faculty member. The faculty are those members of the college or university who have teaching, research, and/or service obligations. The term can be used loosely to include all the instructional staff, including people who have continuing appointments; graduate students who teach courses; and people who teach one or two courses but who do not have a continuing appointment. It can be used narrowly to refer only to those who hold specific ranks such as instructors, assistant professors, associate professors, and full professors and who draw their salary from the college or university. When a college or university refers to its faculty as having certain characteristics, you may want to inquire just how the term *faculty* is being defined.

Graduate Associates/Assistants   Graduate assistants/associates are those students, usually studying for a doctoral degree, who are hired by the university to perform specific teaching, research, or administrative responsibilities. Sometimes graduate assistants/associates are referred to as teaching fellows or teaching assistants, research assistants, or administrative associates. Many graduate students earn their way through graduate school by working in these different roles. This kind of work also prepares the students for the responsibilities they will assume when they join the faculty of a college or university.

Lecturer

A number of titles are applied to faculty members. The title of lecturer is usually given to temporary faculty. Lecturer is a flexible title that can apply to an inexperienced or a highly experienced person. At a research university, lecturers usually have a major teaching assignment and little expectation for conducting research or creative scholarship.

Instructor

The term *instructor* is used in two different ways. It is a general term to refer to the person who will be teaching a course. Thus, one says, "The instructor for Sociology 100 is Dr. Smith." The term can also be a faculty title. Especially in fields where faculty are hired after completing a master's degree, faculty can begin their employment at the rank of instructor.

Assistant Professor

The title of assistant professor is the entry-level rank for most faculty who have a Ph.D.

Associate Professor

The title of associate professor is the second-level rank for most faculty who have the Ph.D. This title recognizes significant accomplishments in teaching, research, and contribution to the profession. Usually faculty with the rank of associate professor have had at least six or seven years of experience teaching at the college level.

Full Professor   The title of full professor, sometimes simply professor, is the highest academic rank for college and university faculty. At a research university, the title connotes leadership in teaching and curriculum development, a record of scholarship that is nationally recognized, leadership in one's professional organization, and often an international reputation.

Chaired Professor   At many colleges and universities, certain outstanding faculty are appointed to named professorships. These appointments are enhanced beyond the usual level of support through gifts to the college or university. Chairs or named professorships usually are made in recognition of a distinguished career. They provide the faculty member with additional resources that can be used to support graduate students, scholarship, professional travel, and other professional activities.

STUDENT CONDUCT

Code of Student Conduct   Most colleges and universities have a code of student conduct. The code is written to protect the rights and property of individuals within the campus community. It is a supplement to the city, state, county, and federal laws that govern each person on the campus. As part of the code, violations are reviewed and sanctions are imposed through a judicial process.

Privacy Act The Family Educational Rights and Privacy Act establishes the privacy of student records and the conditions under which students and others may review a student's educational records.

Academic Misconduct A general term to refer to any behavior that undermines the academic integrity of the institution or disrupts the educational process. Examples include giving information to or receiving information from another student during a test, using the work of someone else and representing it as one's own, or falsifying results of laboratory experiments or data analysis.

Plagiarism Representing the ideas or work of someone else as one's own. This includes a failure to give the reference for words or paragraphs that were taken from another source; it also includes attributing a novel idea to oneself rather than giving credit to the actual source.

HONORS / PLACEMENT

Honors Many colleges and universities have honors programs for undergraduates. The more selective the institution, the less likely it is to have a separate honors program. Honors students usually are identified by their scores on the admissions tests and high school grades or, after admission, by their grades in college courses. Each institution's honors program is distinct. Usually it involves special seminars for honors students taught by faculty who are particularly effective with bright undergraduate students. Certain courses may have special sections for honors students that present the course material in a more challenging way. Often honors programs provide opportunities for students to participate in research and work on independent projects with faculty. Students who are enrolled in honors courses throughout their undergraduate programs usually graduate with an indication of honors on their diplomas.

Placement Tests

After admitting students to the college or university, many institutions administer their own placement tests. Often this takes place during freshman orientation, before classes start. Placement tests help college advisors determine the level of course work the student is ready to attempt. The most common subjects are English, mathematics, and languages. Based on test performance, a student may be advised to take some remedial or precollege-level course work or to move past the entry-level courses into some that are more advanced.

Advanced Placement

Many students take advanced placement courses during high school and then take standardized advanced placement tests in specific subjects. The advanced placement test gives an indication of a student's performance in comparison to college students' performance. Each college and university has its own approach to recognizing advanced placement test results. In some cases, a student can receive course credit for subject areas in which he or she scored exceptionally high. In other cases, the score on the advanced placement test is used to determine which courses the student should take during the first year. The faculty of a college may review a student's examination to determine if credit will be given.

COURSES

Lecture   Many college courses are described as lecture courses. This means that a relatively large number of students take the course and that the primary method of instruction is lecturing. Students in a lecture course expect to have relatively little interaction with the instructor during the class time.

Seminar   Seminar courses involve a relatively small number of students and an instructor. The primary method of instruction is class discussion; critical analysis of material; and, often, student presentations.

Discussion   Many lecture courses have discussion sessions associated with them. During the discussion sessions, students actively talk about the material in the course, present and consider different points of view, and ask questions about ideas or information. Often students are assigned to a discussion section, which they are expected to attend in addition to the basic lectures.

Laboratory   Most courses in the biological and physical sciences, and some courses in the social sciences, involve laboratory sections. Sometimes the laboratory is linked to a lecture course. At the more advanced level, a course may be taught primarily through the laboratory method. Laboratory courses involve students in direct manipulation of materials, experimentation, analysis of data, and reporting of results.

Term Paper   Usually considered to be a substantial assignment, the term paper is assigned at the beginning of the term with a completion date toward the end of the term. This type of assignment is intended to provide the student with ample opportunity to develop an idea, explore a wide range of references on the topic, and analyze the problem or topic based on a variety of sources.

Final Exams Exams given at the end of the term that cover the basic concepts of the material presented in the course. Students usually have a period of time dedicated to final exams when the regularly scheduled classes do not meet. These exams are often two hours in length.

Hour Exams Exams given during the term, usually one class period in length. Instructors vary in the number of hour exams they expect students to take. Usually the hour exams cover course material that was presented during one segment of the course. Sometimes the hour exam is referred to as a mid-term exam when it comes about halfway through the term.

Semester System Many colleges and universities are on the semester system. This means that the academic calendar is divided into two equal parts, sometimes separated by a winter or Christmas holiday and sometimes with final exams two or three weeks after Christmas vacation or winter break. Semesters can be from fourteen to sixteen weeks long. A course that is given during one semester is worth a certain number of credit hours. Most courses are offered for three credit hours; but if the course meets more often and the student is required to do extensive laboratory or field work, the course can be offered for more than three credit hours. The number of credits associated with any single course varies widely from one department to another and from one college to another. An average load is fifteen credit hours per semester. The University of Michigan, Georgetown University, and Harvard University use the semester system. About 75 percent of colleges and universities operate with a semester system.

Quarter System Some colleges and universities are on the quarter system. This means that the academic calendar is divided into four ten- or eleven-week quarters. Students are usually enrolled for three quarters per year, but they can be enrolled year round if the courses they need for their program are offered in the summer. A course offered during a quarter is worth a certain number of credits. Many courses are offered for three credits, but others can be offered for four, five, or more depending on the amount of time involved. As a rule of thumb, three semester credit hours is the equivalent of five quarter credit hours. This information is particularly important if a student transfers from an institution on the quarter system to one on the semester system or vice versa. Stanford University and The Ohio State University use the quarter system. About 25 percent of colleges and universities operate with a quarter system.

FINANCIAL AID

Student Financial Aid Financial aid is available to help students finance their education when their own personal and family resources are not adequate to cover the costs. The three basic types of financial aid are scholarships and grants (assistance that does not have to be repaid), loans (at varying rates of interest that do need to be repaid), and part-time employment on campus. Some colleges have cooperative housing where students work in exchange for a room and board as another form of financial aid. Colleges and universities have professional staff to counsel students about the types of aid for which they are eligible and to process financial aid packages. Aid can be awarded on the basis of family financial resources as well as on the basis of academic merit or special talent. Most colleges believe that families have the primary responsibility to finance postsecondary education. Financial aid is available to help meet the difference between what families can provide, what the student can earn, and what it costs to attend college. Most forms of aid require students to be enrolled full time (at least twelve quarter hours or ten semester hours).

Financial Aid Form   The Financial Aid Form (FAF) is a detailed analysis of the student's financial resources as well as the family's resources. It is used by colleges, the federal government, and the states to determine eligibility for certain forms of aid. Most colleges require the completion of the FAF before processing a student's financial aid package or making recommendations about scholarships and loans.

Work Study   Work study is a form of federally subsidized financial aid. Students qualify on the basis of financial need and may apply for various jobs on campus. They are paid an hourly wage and are allocated a total number of hours per year. The funds to cover their salaries come in part from the federal government and in part from the college or university. The idea behind work study is that students find employment in campus offices and that they arrange their work hours to complement their classroom and study times.

STUDENT SUPPORT SERVICES

Academic Advisor   All students are assigned an academic advisor who may be either a faculty member, a professional advisor, or a graduate student. Students are expected to meet with the advisor to plan out their programs of study so that college requirements and the requirements of a major are fulfilled. Academic advisors are available to help students make academic decisions, to help resolve academic problems, and to plan a program of study that will be best suited to the student's personal and career goals.

Residence Hall Counselor   Colleges and universities employ upper-level undergraduates, graduate students, or other professionals to live in the residence halls and help students with the problems and challenges of daily life. Most residence halls have a director who supervises all aspects of the residence hall and residence hall counselors who are assigned to each floor or wing. The counselors help students resolve conflicts, ensure that rules and regulations of the residence hall are followed, and promote positive social interactions. Often residence hall counselors also help students think about academic problems they are facing.

Counseling Center In addition to the academic advisors and the residence hall counselors, most colleges and universities have a counseling center. This student service provides in-depth career counseling, short-term therapy for students who are having emotional problems, and crisis intervention for students who confront serious life crises and emotional disorganization. Most counseling centers sponsor support groups of different types, offer workshops on many aspects of personal growth and development, and help students expand the ability to cope with the many challenges of adult life.

Student Health Center The student health center provides basic health services. Usually students pay a modest fee for services or purchase a health insurance policy that includes access to the student health service. The student health center can administer medications, diagnose and treat many illnesses, and refer students who need more specialized medical treatment. Many student health centers also offer programs in fitness, wellness, illness prevention, and educational programs about health-related concerns.

Disability Services Many colleges and universities have offices to assist students who have some type of physical disability. The staff members are trained to assess disabilities, including learning disabilities; to help students negotiate the physical environment of the campus; and to provide appropriate assistance in meeting course requirements. Many learning disabilities are diagnosed for the first time at the college level when a student's typical strategies for compensating for a disability are no longer adequate because of the amount of work required.

Minority Affairs   Most campuses have one or more offices that provide supportive programs for minority students. Minority students include African American, Asian American, native American, and Hispanic students. In some regions, Appalachian students are considered a minority group. Programming can range broadly, including cultural enrichment, academic support, leadership development, career exploration, social organizations, service organizations, financial aid services, and individual counseling.

STUDENT LIFE

Student Government   Student government is the elected body of students who provide leadership for the campus. Student government usually is an important vehicle for supporting the development of student organizations, representing student opinion in important campus committees, and providing an avenue for the expression of student opinion on major new initiatives or campus problems that affect students.

Greek System   The fraternities and sororities associated with a college or university are called the Greek system since most of them use Greek letters for their names. Each chapter is affiliated with the college but is operated independently from the college. Fraternities and sororities are usually, but not always, affiliated with a national organization that determines many of the policies, rules and procedures, and responsibilities of the local chapter. Fraternities and sororities have to abide by certain campus rules and regulations; but the residences, the regulations about membership, the fees, and other aspects of the organization are determined by the local chapter and the national organization. Not all colleges and universities have a Greek system, and not all fraternities and sororities are represented on every college campus.

Greek Council   This is a governmental council made up of representatives of the fraternities and sororities. They meet in regular sessions and determine policies related to the Greek system on a specific campus. They also serve as a judicial body to hear cases concerning rules violations by member chapters or individual members and to decide on punishments or sanctions. Usually, the Greek council operates with college supervision or monitoring. On some campuses, separate interfraternity and intersorority councils perform these functions.

Rush   This is the system through which new members are added to the fraternities and sororities. The rush calendar is determined by the Greek council in conjunction with the college administration. Rush procedures differ from campus to campus. The purpose, however, is always the same—to recruit new members who are compatible with the other members of the group. Students who decide to rush usually sign up formally. The rush system acquaints potential members with the Greek system in general as well as with a particular house. Rushees are usually required to attend open houses at a specified number of fraternities or sororities on campus and often must have cards signed indicating they have complied with the requirement. At these functions, rushees get to know some of the members and get to know where the houses are. They often receive a tour of the house at this time. Rush parties are social functions designed to show the potential member how a particular group likes to socialize. At the end of the rush period, Greek houses extend bids to people they hope will join them. Some rushees may receive bids to join more than one house, others may receive no bids at all. After bids come out, rushees have a specified amount of time to declare their intentions. Most fraternities and sororities assign big brothers or big sisters who act as special friends and advisors to the new recruits.

Pledge   After accepting a bid to become a member of a house on campus, the rushee becomes a pledge. The group of people entering a house in a particular year is known as the pledge class. A pledgemaster is a member of the house who is assigned to supervise the pledges' activities. The activities usually include work parties, learning the history of the chapter and the national organization, and participating in secret rituals. Pledge procedures vary from campus to campus. In most cases, the serious hazing (exposure to harassment or ridicule) that was characteristic of pledging in years gone by has been outlawed, but the pledge is still expected to show certain signs of support for the organization during the pledge period. Pledges may also be required to wear a pledge pin or some other symbol of their status and affiliation. The pledge period is designed to cement the potential member's allegiance to the house. Pledging ends with admission to full brotherhood or sisterhood. This used to occur at an initiation ceremony at the conclusion of Hell Night—a night of special testing of the pledge's commitment to the chapter. Now this procedure may be more dignified and less frightening.

Commuter Student

Many colleges have minimal or no residential facilities. Almost all the students commute to the campus for their courses. On campuses that do have residential facilities, those students who have to drive to campus or take public transportation are often referred to as commuter students. For commuter students, important considerations about a college are the availability and cost of parking facilities, the availability of study space and places for social interaction, and the availability of classes during the later afternoon, evening, and weekend hours.

Nontraditional Student

All students who enter or attend college who are older than the typical eighteen- to twenty-two-year old, students who have children, students who have been in the labor market for several years and are now starting college, veterans, or students who are returning to college to make a career change are considered nontraditional students. Some colleges and universities have special enrollment units for nontraditional students. Advisors may be trained specially to help adults make academic decisions in light of their changing career goals or to help students coordinate their work, family, and academic responsibilities.

1 | The Changing Parent-Child Relationship

*W*hen we began teaching college, we were in our late twenties. Our oldest child was two. We had just finished writing a book about human development and our heads were filled with the findings of the research literature. Looking back we realize that we had few life experiences to fill in the gaps. In one evening course on human development, several of the students were in their fifties and sixties. During the class devoted to middle adulthood, we lectured on retirement from parenthood. We pointed out the similarities to retirement from employment, identified the importance of the shift in energy to new roles, and described changes in the marriage relationship when children leave home.

A kindly looking man in the class smiled all through the lecture. It seemed as though we were really making a big impression on him. When the lecture was over, he raised his hand and said, "You know, as far as I'm concerned, you never retire from parenthood. Those kids are a part of my life and part of my worries as long as I'm alive." Of course, he was right.

That remark brought back a flood of memories of our relationships with our parents during the years we were in college. We remembered looking forward to letters from home and care packages of brownies and cookies; worrying whether we would disappoint our parents when we decided to transfer from prestigious eastern colleges to a large, midwestern university; wanting some sign of support from our parents when we were deciding to go on to study for our Ph.D.s. We remembered how important our parents were to us. Even when we disagreed with them, their voices sounded clearly in our minds. Our perceptions of their opinions and reactions were major influences in our decision making.

Now we have come to appreciate how difficult it is for parents to send their children off to college. As a parent, you want to encourage your child to build a future filled with new opportunities. You sense your child's need to exercise independent judgment and to make decisions. You hope your child will be able to do well without your constant protection and supervision. Yet the college environment is a large, unknown quantity. There are probably no family friends or relatives to look out for your child at college. There may be stories of unconventional ideas and social excesses. College may be far away, too far for a weekend visit. Even if college is nearby, your child may be too busy to spend much time with you.

You know that once your child goes off to college, you will never have the same feelings of closeness and family togetherness you had while he or she was living at home. This is a turning point, a time of irreversible change. You have planned for it, talked about it, and saved for it. You have great pride in being able to provide this opportunity for your child, and you have great pride in your child's achievements. Yet it is a bittersweet time, a time for encouraging someone you love to move on, and a time for missing that child. You must begin to overcome the negative feelings and face the opportunities that this period of life presents.

It is natural to want to understand this period in your lives and theirs so that you can continue to help as best you can, and so that you can continue your own positive, psychological growth. The first step is to understand what changes in the parent-child relationship can be expected over the next few years.

ACHIEVING AUTONOMY THROUGH MUTUAL RESPECT

When children are young, parents are preoccupied with three essential functions: 1) to protect children by looking out for their health and safety; 2) to nurture children by giving them sustenance, affection, support, encouragement for their sense of joy in life, and avenues through which they may attain a sense of mastery; and 3) to socialize children by teaching them ways to behave appropriately and values to help guide their behavior. Through our behavior, our discipline practices, and our explanations, we help them adapt to society as we know it. We impart a sense of values and beliefs that reflects our best understanding of what it means to be a mature, successful member of the community.

As parents, we are charged with a singularly difficult task—to give our children both roots and wings. Our job is to build a sense of closeness, security, and trust within the family group. At the same time, we must do all we can to help children leave our family and live independently as adults, both singly and, for most, in a new family of their making.

Parents accept these seemingly contradictory goals, building closeness and fostering independence, with various emphases and levels of reflection. The art of parenting involves balancing these goals so well that children feel valued and secure in their families *and* confident as they move independently in the world, eager for the challenges and opportunities of life.

As our children get older, we protect less and worry more. Parents of college-age children often view this time as the hardest for the children and the hardest for them. Most parents recognize that for children to achieve independence, they must have the freedom to make decisions on their own. With this freedom comes the responsibility of living with mistakes. As adults, and especially as parents, most of us are very uncomfortable with mistakes. We have learned the importance of being correct. There is little room for poor judgment or failures in reasoning at work, at home, and in our communities. People count on us to make good decisions.

College students are really just beginners in the game of critical life decision making. They do not have the experience to anticipate some of the consequences of their choices. They will make more mistakes at this time than later because they are learning to live on their own. It is natural to make more errors during the early phases of learning any new role. Only by making decisions and mistakes from time to time can they take full responsibility for their decisions. Young adults need opportunities to fail occasionally in order to learn what we have taken twenty years to learn.

Unfortunately, some of their errors in judgment and choice can be costly, not only financially but for their health and well-being. Most parents of college students face the critical conflict of how to give children the room they need to experiment and explore and still prevent the serious consequences of their mistakes. We do not know much about what is going on when they are at college, and the opportunities for interaction are limited. We wonder how we can protect them from disastrous mistakes and still convey the sense that we have confidence in their ability to make good decisions.

One approach to this dilemma is to examine the course that your child has followed up to this point in striving for independence. Most young people begin their surge for independence at a behavioral level. Children try to demonstrate that they are distinct from their parents through their choice of clothing or hair styles, the expression of individual tastes in music, or the use of slang expressions that are unfamiliar to their parents. Family arguments often focus on behavioral issues such as coming home after curfew, talking too long on the telephone, spending too much money, or giving too little time to schoolwork.

Although these arguments are unpleasant, the conflicts do not really reflect a substantial rift in the parent-child relationship. Most children who engage in these kinds of conflicts still respect their family's values and rules. They try to establish a bit more power for themselves by making day-to-day decisions and asserting their own needs and wants, tastes and preferences.

The high school years provide important evidence about your child's ability to make independent decisions and to reason through difficult situations. You know how often and in what areas your child made choices that you did not approve of or thought were wrong. To the extent that you have trusted your child to exercise good judgment and have been proud of his or her decisions, you should approach the college years with optimism.

The achievement of autonomy moves in some new directions during the college years. In addition to engaging in a wide range of new behaviors, young adults begin to seek emotional autonomy and, to some degree, value autonomy from their parents. College students' willingness to experience their parents' disapproval reflects their desire for emotional autonomy. Young adults will say, "I know my parents don't approve of this, but I think they are wrong so I am going to do it anyway." Young adults gain a new confidence in their own judgment. They believe, correctly or incorrectly, that they have the ability to evaluate a situation and to reach a conclusion different from one their parents might have drawn. They test the limits of their emotional autonomy by risking parental disapproval.

Movement toward autonomy of values comes even later than emotional autonomy. Through most of the young adult years, beginning at about age eighteen and continuing into the twenties, a person evaluates, extends, corrects, and expresses basic values and standards. Value development is stimulated by college courses such as philosophy, ethics, psychology, and sociology, where values are systematically analyzed. Value exploration is a natural part of the psychological process of identity formation.

Young adults begin to express commitments to life goals that may be quite distinct from commitments their parents have made. Many parents did not attend college, but they want their children to have the opportunity. They may not anticipate that a college education will do more than open the door to occupational opportunities—it will influence a child's world view. Children of labor union supporters may decide to become managers or entrepreneurs. Children of business men and women may choose careers in social services. Children of pacifists may decide to join the military. Children of teachers may decide to become corporate executives. The commitments you have made to family, career, and community that make up the structure of your adulthood may not be your children's choices.

These important new steps in achieving independence may not be entirely comfortable for college students or for their parents. Most college students are not ready to be completely independent. They still depend on their parents for financial support. They still want to feel that their family is a secure base to which they can return for nurturing and a sense of belonging. At the same time, students feel an urgency about establishing an independent, internal standard for making decisions and guiding their behavior. One young woman stated it this way:

> I'm beginning to start a life of my own with a little help from my friends. And it hurts drawing away from my mother. At times, I'm almost overcome, yearning for that time of perfect knowledge between the two of us. . . . I don't want to try to get even with her, and I hope this distance between us isn't permanent. As soon as I feel like a unique person, unique and separate from her, then those boundaries will be enough and I can relax the artificial ones. (Goethals and Klos, 1986, pp. 40–41)

Along with the waves of pride in their child's emerging autonomy, most parents feel pangs of rejection from time to time as they experience their child's indifference or emotional distance. Some parents may view the child's movement toward emotional and value autonomy as defiance, rebellion, or ingratitude. Some parents really miss the feelings of intimacy and closeness they had with their child when he or she was younger. This is natural. You have spent a long period of your adult life protecting and nurturing your child. Your emotional reactions signal the change in this relationship. They prompt you to begin thinking about your own future and goals. Autonomy is a two-way street. As your child gains independence, so do you.

You can begin to appreciate how important movement toward autonomy is when you consider that you and your children have overlapping but not identical futures. The choices and commitments you made during your twenties took you forward into your adulthood. You made the best choices you could with your knowledge about the past and present and your anticipation of the future. You still have choices to make and commitments to fulfill for the period of your life that lies ahead.

Your children's commitments anticipate an adulthood that will unfold into the twenty-first century. They must adapt to a future different from the one you faced when you were twenty-two. One of the tasks of parenting is to foster your children's ability to survive beyond your own lifetime. Perhaps it is easier to understand and support their need to explore new goals as you realize this.

You can begin to explore your own future as you gain confidence in your child's ability to carve out a meaningful life. As you spend less of your energy and resources meeting your children's needs, you can begin to reflect on aspects of your own talents and goals that have been neglected or not yet identified. You may be willing to take some new risks and to set out on some new paths now that your children do not rely on you as they once did for their daily protection, guidance, and care. More and more people are living to be one hundred years old. With this view of a possible future, you may want to reassess your own life goals and move off in some new directions.

Most people are in the period of middle adulthood (approximately thirty-four to sixty) when their children are in college. The primary tasks of development in this period of adult life are nurturing the marriage relationship, managing the household, parenting, and managing a career (Newman and Newman, 1991). With less time required for parenting as a child attends college, couples are likely to rediscover the pleasures and rewards of their relationship with one another. They may also discover new facets of their own talents and interests that make them more intriguing to one another as partners. A few evenings of listening to favorite records, ordering a pizza just for the two of you, or sitting together enjoying a new kind of quiet may lead gradually to a redirection of energy from nurturing your child to nurturing your marriage.

For some adults this is not possible. They are already divorced or widowed by the time their children leave for college. Some families have a number of younger children, so the family environment is not changed that much when the first child begins college. However, the desire and capacity for new, deeper levels of intimacy that are likely to emerge during middle adulthood can be satisfied in a variety of ways. Adults may reach out to form new friendships or bring a new kind of openness to former friendships. Some adults channel this sense of caring into love relationships, others into close mentoring relationships at work, and still others find renewed intimacy with a sibling or other family member.

In addition to achieving new levels of intimacy, adults find that their home and life-style become a focus for new attention and energy. If other children are still at home, parents may discover that the lessons learned with their older child help them become more successful in managing a redefined, downsized household. There is a bit more time to spend interacting with the younger children; often a new feeling of space in a home not occupied to the hilt; and a slightly lighter load of day-to-day tasks—less laundry, fewer dishes, smaller meals to prepare, fewer incoming phone calls to answer and messages to take, fewer school events to coordinate, and fewer fights among the siblings to referee. All is not heaven of course, but there is a bit more time to take a look at changing some things about the way you use your home—adding a new flower bed in the yard, using the basement room in a new way, or setting up an office area in part of the spare bedroom. You may not have a lot of new financial resources, since those are all going to pay for the costs of college; but you will have some new resources in time, space, and energy.

Time begins to come under your own discretion a bit more, especially if one child is at college and the others are in high school. This means a chance to become involved in new aspects of your work setting, to engage in new community activities, or to take on new leadership roles. The financial burdens of paying for a child's college education may lead to a new investment in career advancement or to taking on additional work through part-time employment, consultation, or home-based projects. One avenue that often opens up for people is the opportunity to train and supervise younger workers. This direction provides a new form of nurturing, in some ways replacing the energy that had been directed toward parenting. Supervisors who are able to transfer some of the concern they have for their children to socializing and training younger workers can make a meaningful and lasting contribution to the development of young professionals.

College students struggle to develop a sense of personal identity, a concept we will discuss in greater depth in chapter 2. For middle adults, the comparable struggle involves developing a sense of generativity—a commitment to improving the quality of life for future generations. Every society counts on those who have reached

middle adulthood to use some of their energy and resources to improve conditions for future generations. If
individuals in middle adulthood exhaust the resources of
the land, fail to pass on the knowledge of the culture, or
become so preoccupied with their own pleasures and
power that they do not look after the well-being of the
young, the society as a whole cannot survive. The conflict
of middle adulthood is to be able to achieve a sense of
responsibility that goes beyond "me and mine" to a sense
of community.

Children provide one concrete source of evidence about
adults' impact on the future. Activities that generate new
products, new ideas, or a new sense of community provide
other evidence. New efforts at work to improve the quality
of what is achieved, to develop more capable workers, or
to extend the services of the workplace to those who are in
need are all ways to satisfy the desire to achieve a sense of
generativity. People may turn their attention to global
concerns, to political issues, protection of the environment,
nuclear disarmament, world hunger, or peace. Adults can
express generativity in a wide variety of ways. The important point is for them to contribute to a future that extends
beyond their immediate needs and the needs of their family members. One element in this process is giving our
children the freedom to carve out their own future, one
that is distinct from our unfulfilled dreams or our vision of
their future.

THE PARADOX OF
AUTONOMY AND CLOSENESS

One of the challenges for us as parents is to help our
children build autonomy while we build confidence in

their judgment. You can contribute to this emerging autonomy by gradually replacing your automatic advice and opinions with invitations for them to use their own ideas and to seek advice from you as needed. Try to strengthen your child's ability to rely on reasoning and problem-solving skills in making choices and plans. Encourage the use of various sources of information to reach a decision. Talk with your child about the possible consequences of one course of action compared with another. Help consider the tradeoffs involved in making choices.

Involve your children in family decision making when it seems appropriate. Give them information about the important decisions the family is facing, let them hear how you are approaching these decisions, and ask for their advice. When they are at home, let them know your concerns and ask them to help decide what limits or guidelines make sense rather than insisting on strict rules.

As you gradually reduce your role as an agent of socialization and engage your child in reasoned, shared decision making, you will find that you have a new source of ideas and new lines of communication. Young adults who participate actively in family decisions become more confident about the value of their own opinions and ideas. As a result, they may become more willing to disagree with their parents and to openly challenge their views. They will also be more willing to try out ideas with their parents. The benefit of this openness is that parents have greater insight into their children's explorations. Parents may also have a new source of ideas for addressing the problems they face.

As emotional autonomy increases, children will be more confident of their separateness and will have less need to react intensely. College students will disagree with their parents more openly when they do not feel they need to hide from their parents' disapproval. In this dialogue, parents can learn more about the alternatives their children are considering. You must try to remain open-minded and keep your sense of humor during this process. As you become more aware of the way your child approaches decisions, your confidence will build.

Ironically, your child is likely to feel a new sense of closeness with you at the same time as a comfortable level of independence is achieved. Out of the tugging and pulling of different opinions, you will probably discover that you not only understand your child better, but he or she gains a new understanding of you. Your child is likely to gain new respect for you when discussions confirm that you are reasonable and that you are willing to consider new opinions. College students, supported by many, many sources of evidence of their increased independence, begin to voice a new appreciation and admiration for their parents. Once children feel they no longer need to struggle to convince their parents or themselves about their autonomy, they often experience new feelings of connectedness with their parents.

In one college course we taught, students were asked to describe how their relationship with their parents changed from the time they were in high school to the present (most of these students were juniors and seniors). Many students reported that they had grown closer to their parents during the college years. Here are some examples of their responses:

I was very rebellious and I needed to be independent. Since I have left for college, I have mellowed and so have my parents.

[Coming to college] has made our relationship, for the most part, much better. We have become much closer because, it seems, I've grown. Also, they are (in spite of my sometimes absolute failures in college) very proud of me.

Coming to [college] has helped my relationship with my parents. It gave me a broader picture to judge my parents by. Now it is easier to accept my parents as people, not all-powerful beings.

I think my coming to college has improved my relationship with my parents because they are learning to treat me as a capable and responsible adult, not like the baby girl of the family.

Some students are still struggling with their parents, and others remain distant. They say their parents are putting too much pressure on them, that their parents do not seem to respect their judgment, that their parents do not accept their need for independence, or that their parents are indifferent to their needs and problems. Some students expressed these concerns:

Our relationship has changed greatly. They realized that I am my own person and they can't tell me what to do. Since I've been at college, I have let my true self show. My parents sometimes see this as rebellious. We do not always see eye to eye.

Coming to college has distanced my relationship in many ways because they (my parents) don't know exactly what's going on in my life now.

My parents don't understand why I do certain things (i.e., dramatic hair styles and clothing). They like me to tone my "antics" down when I come home. We are a close family. I have not lost touch with them, I've only changed the way I think. I don't run my life for them anymore—I run it for me. This fact irritates them quite a bit.

You can see from these examples that college students are not indifferent to their parents' opinions and views. However, their needs for autonomy may outweigh their needs for parental approval.

Throughout adolescence and adulthood, we strive to achieve autonomy in relation to our parents. Autonomy is not the same as rejection, alienation, financial independence, or physical separation, but is a psychological state in which parents and children accept one another's independent individuality. Young adults and parents who establish autonomy during the college years can recognize both similarities and differences in each other. They do not feel totally absorbed or dominated by one another's goals and expectations. College students who have achieved autonomy do not feel compelled to fulfill parental expectations for their career choices. Parents who have achieved autonomy do not feel tied to their children's expectations that they continue to do the same kind of work, live in the same home, or remain married for their children's sake.

Autonomy does not guarantee a life of perfect agreement and cohesiveness between parents and their adult children. As adults, you probably continue to have differences of opinion with your own parents about many topics, not the least of which is how to raise your adolescent children. At times, adults may even feel that they have become more dependent upon their parents than they were during the college years. This is particularly likely if adults depend on their parents to look after their small children, or if they experience a life crisis such as serious illness, divorce, or unemployment. Adults often turn to their parents as a major source of emotional comfort and financial support during these times.

But what you probably have been striving to achieve in your relationship with your parents, and what you hope you can achieve with your young adult children, is mutual respect. You want to have confidence and pride in your children's advice, judgment, and decision-making skills, and you want them to gain a more realistic appreciation of these qualities in you. This foundation of mutual respect gives your children the strength to pursue their vision of the future and to seek your advice when they need it. It allows you to pursue your own vision of the future, and to turn to your children for their advice when you need it. By nurturing autonomy, you may actually gain a valuable new resource—advice and encouragement from someone who respects and cares about you.

ADDITIONAL READING

Bloom, M. V. (1980). *Adolescent parental separation*. New York: Gardner Press.

Bowlby, J. (1988). *A secure base: Parent-child attachment and healthy human development*. New York: Basic Books.

Coburn, K. L. and Treeger, M. L. (1988). *Letting go: A parents' guide to today's college experience*. Bethesda, MD: Adler and Adler.

Shields, C. J. (1988). *The college guide for parents* (rev. ed.) New York: College Entrance Examination Board.

Identity
Formation

Young people work hard to establish a personal identity during the college years. They worry about their essential character in much the same way that five- and six-year-old children struggle with questions about life and death. They ask themselves, Who am I? What do I stand for? What do I want in life?

Young people must take into account the bonds that have been built with others in the past as well as the directions for new relationships they hope to form in the future as they try to define themselves. Personal identity requires that young people understand their unique qualities and how they fit into the surrounding social environment. They merge personal qualities and goals with the expectations and demands of family, friends, community, and culture. Their personal identities serve as anchor points that allow them to experience continuity in social relationships.

Erik Erikson (1959) describes the achievement of personal identity:

> The young individual must learn to be most himself where he means the most to others—those others, to be sure, who have come to mean most to him. The term *identity* expresses such a mutual relation in that it connotes both a persistent sameness within oneself (self-sameness) and a persistent sharing of some kind of essential character with others. (p. 102)

Personal identity takes shape as young adults select certain roles and reject others, make commitments to certain values and goals and reject others. Through self-conscious, personal reflection, young adults become increasingly aware of their own interests, needs, and values. They also become aware of the expectations of their society, including the way their culture defines successful maturity. In order to achieve personal identity, individuals must integrate their interests, talents, and goals with socially acceptable roles and values.

Most college students put effort into clarifying their personal goals and commitments. They try to tie their commitments to past and current achievements in order to decide what they are good at and what they care about. To create an identity, a person must spend time, reflect, explore, and be willing to tolerate periods of uncertainty. Personal identity serves as a map to guide important life decisions about career selection, marriage, religion, and moral and political values.

Personal identity is not a fixed structure that is finalized during the college years. Adulthood is filled with events that could not be experienced and opportunities that were not anticipated during the years from eighteen to twenty-two. Adults enter new roles—marriage partner, parent, supervisor of others, community leader—that call for talents and abilities that were not recognized earlier. People may encounter life crises such as illness, divorce, or the death of a loved one that limit choices and challenge values. People may take another look at their commitments and begin to explore new directions after they reach goals established during the early years of adulthood. Identity evolves in adulthood as experiences cause people to review, revise, and extend their knowledge of themselves.

The first draft of personal identity usually emerges, however, as students encounter the diversity and demands of the college environment. This draft provides a vision of the self in the future that guides young adults' initial decisions about career, marriage, religion, ethics, and participation in the community and the energy for sustained activity to realize this vision.

THE ROLE OF THE PAST IN IDENTITY DEVELOPMENT

A person's identity is built on elements of the past, present, and future. People review significant identifications with others in the past. Young children usually look up to their parents, older brothers and sisters, some important relatives, teachers, religious leaders, and community leaders. Young children actively strive to enhance their self-concepts by incorporating some of the valued characteristics of these people into their own behavior. This is called identification.

You probably remember when your children thought you were the most important, powerful, and perfect person on earth. Most children think their parents are ideal people. They want to become like these ideal people, and so they imitate their parents' behaviors, repeat things their parents say, and accept their parents' values as good and right for them.

Young children also achieve a sense of safety and security by taking on their parents' qualities through identification. They feel they have their parents' valuable qualities inside them even when they are separated from their parents. Children use their identifications to help guide their behavior and achieve a sense of confidence.

As your children became teenagers, you probably noticed that you toppled somewhat from this position of unquestioned admiration. You may even have become the target of scorn. Teens review their past identifications and evaluate their heroes and heroines. They begin to sort out how they feel about people who have been important in their lives. They begin to realize how they are different from their idols. By doing this they achieve emotional independence. To develop a strong, positive sense of self, young adults must attain emotional independence and discover ideas and feelings of well-being that are their own. College students will sort through the important relationships they have developed and reflect on the qualities of people they admire. As their values and goals become clearer, they will continue to admire some qualities of these early figures and discard others.

A college student may say that she is proud of her father because of the important role he plays in the community and the amount of time he has given to his church. She may also say, however, that he is not as successful a businessman as he might have been and that she wishes he would be more competitive. In this way, she is creating a more complex picture of her father than she had as a child. She may try to include the traits she values in her own personal identity. She may also be critical of some qualities and try to improve on what she perceives as her father's weaknesses.

Forming a personal identity involves reviewing family history and childhood identifications. Each family creates a personal history that reflects the family's ancestry, religion, race, country of origin, and some specific mythology or folklore about the triumphs and the crises of past generations. The family history is handed down in different ways from one generation to the next. You may pass it on through photo albums, celebrations, visits to grave sites, favorite stories about family members, religious beliefs, a style of cooking, and a particular use of language.

Most college students express an interest in discovering more about their personal history. They may begin to ask new questions about your family's past. You may find that your son or daughter wants to know even more than you do about your family's history. You may notice a renewed interest in family traditions, new questions about family beliefs, and a new commitment to carry on elements of the past that have been lost or ignored.

Students find new resources in the college environment to help them pursue answers to some of their questions about personal history. A Jewish student, for example, may enroll in a course in Yiddish to retrieve an important element of personal history. A black student may take a course in African American literature or African culture to learn more about his or her cultural tradition. A student with French ancestry may enroll in a study tour to visit the area of France where family members lived. College is an ideal setting in which to raise and explore questions about the traditions, myths, contributions, and struggles of various peoples, religions, and cultures.

Using the resources of the college, students can piece

together some clues about their personal past. They are likely to spend creative energy rummaging through fragments of information about their history, religion, and culture in putting together a more complete picture of their personal past. Many faculty members recognize the strong need for students to comprehend their past. Where possible, they build on their motivation by giving students opportunities to write papers and to explore the literature on topics that will help shed more light on these issues.

In one human development course, for example, students complete a major assignment in which they interview members of three generations of a family. Most students choose to interview members of their own families. They describe the specific challenges that each person faces and any themes that show continuity across the three generations. Students discover that they understand their own values and goals more clearly as they learn how these values have been transmitted from their grandparents' or great-grandparents' generations. They also begin to appreciate how their own futures will be similar in some ways and different in others from those of their grandparents' and parents' generations.

THE ROLE OF THE PRESENT IN IDENTITY DEVELOPMENT

The present, as well as the past, contributes information and ideas that shape personal identity. The most important information students gather in the present is about their talents, interests, needs, and values. Human talents are diverse. Just think of all the different ways people contribute to their families, their communities, and their nations. Analytic skills, creative talents, social and interpersonal talents, talents for innovation and invention, technical expertise, and talents in athletics and the performing arts are just a few ways individuals contribute to social life.

During college young adults uncover their talents and interests. They can refine their skills and knowledge in fields they encountered during high school, or they can explore subjects they have never studied before. Universities offer a wide range of subjects, many of which are not available in high school curricula. Even in fields where courses are offered in high school, like mathematics, history, or foreign language, the range of special topics covered at the college level brings the student into contact with a new view of the scope of the subject and new demands for thinking and problem solving. Within such a context, young people can begin to clarify what they do well, what they enjoy, and those talents and skills they intend to develop.

College and university faculty, administrators, and staff understand students' critical needs to discover their talents and to build a sense of confidence about their abilities. They also understand that this process requires some experimentation and exposure to various ways of thinking. This is precisely why most colleges have an undergraduate curriculum with a full range of disciplines and perspectives. No matter what field a student intends to study, most colleges require students to sample broadly from the basic areas and approaches to knowledge including the social sciences, the natural sciences, mathematics, language and literature, the humanities, and the arts. This structure can be a powerful mechanism for fostering individual growth when it is used to its full advantage. Students begin to discover the styles of problem raising and problem solving that are used in different fields. They learn about the contributions people in various fields have made to society. They have opportunities to try their hand at solving problems from many different perspectives.

Through this process, students clarify their talents and interests and identify what they do exceptionally well. Students may strengthen their convictions to pursue talents they identified in high school. They may discover an even closer fit between their interests and certain special areas within a field they had been attracted to earlier. In many cases, students find that they have talents and interests they never recognized or valued before college. This is a wonderful insight that gives a person a new sense of pride and commitment to the future.

Kathy is a young woman who went to high school with our son Sam. When she started college, she intended to study biology and expressed interest in becoming a microbiologist. Her father taught science in middle school, and she had always excelled in her science courses. She entered an honors program at the university and began to take a variety of liberal arts courses. One seminar in history and another in psychology were especially interesting to her. Over the next two years she struggled with her decision making, vacillating between interests in science, psychology, philosophy, and history. She continued to enroll in honors seminars in history. One of her professors was especially encouraging and invited her to participate in a special military history project. By the end of her junior year, history was it. She expressed a new sense of personal satisfaction with her decision and a new level of enthusiasm about her studies. Now she is considering graduate study in history. She sees her work in history as valuable and exciting in its own right, and she is beginning to sense that she has the ability to make some original contributions to the field.

A major step in self-definition occurs when a young person can express confidence in his or her talents and interests. Confidence produces a constantly renewed sense of hope about being able to make valuable contributions. Parents play an important role in recognizing and encouraging their children's accomplishments. As a parent, you understand your children's abilities better than anyone. You have seen them approach and cope with a variety of academic, social, and extracurricular challenges. You are aware of their accomplishments and failures.

At the same time, you know other adults well. You are aware of the kinds of talents they use to reach their life goals. You can provide support and encouragement for the directions your child is taking. You can also offer a perspective on the real demands of marriage, work, and parenting. You are aware of the kinds of resources and talents needed to balance these critical life roles successfully.

You hope your children will find a good match between their talents and interests and a career in which they can develop their talents. The search may be slow. It requires a great deal of self-understanding and an awareness of the many possible alternatives. As parents, you can reassure your children during periods of uncertainty and discouragement. Let them know you understand that they are facing a difficult problem that may take some time to solve. You can point to the many talents and skills they have discovered during earlier periods of life. You can offer encouragement about the promise of developing these talents further and of discovering new abilities as they face new challenges.

Often, college provides diverse personal contacts as well as a diverse curriculum. The change from high school to college usually brings students into contact with other students from around the state, from other states, and, in some cases, from other countries. Many colleges and universities recruit students from various racial, ethnic, and life-style backgrounds to reflect the diversity of the nation's population. These institutions believe that diversity provides a richness to the students' social contacts and contributes to the creation of a socially and intellectually stimulating environment. Consequently, each student has opportunities to appreciate the similarities and differences that exist in personal beliefs, attitudes, and life goals among a diverse group of students. Students gain an understanding of the differences in customs and values. They build a framework to reflect upon and evaluate their own attitudes and beliefs by talking with other students about their life experiences and hopes for the future.

Of course some colleges bring together a homogeneous student body by recruiting students who share common religious beliefs, philosophical orientations, and life goals. Some colleges see their mission as serving a local population or a particular racial or ethnic group. These colleges may provide a climate that is intended to nurture rather than challenge their students' world views. Nonetheless, all colleges attempt to promote independent thinking, which causes students to reexamine their earlier views.

A VIEW OF THE FUTURE
AND IDENTITY DEVELOPMENT

The third component of personal identity is clarifying a view of the future. It is not quite enough to know where you have come from and what you do well. A meaningful personal identity provides guidance about the directions your life should take.

As one student described it, "I want to become someone, someone who is valued and accepted by myself and by others. I want to make a contribution, to have an impact, to make a difference in this world."

Forming a personal identity involves learning to make commitments. Commitments are promises or pledges to direct our energy, our resources, and our attention to certain values, goals, and relationships. They require a psychological investment in a view of the future. As a result of making a commitment, a person will persist in an activity or a relationship over a long period of time. Once a commitment is made, the psychological investment required to achieve a goal or build a relationship motivates a person to work hard and to endure failures and hardships. Commitment sustains a person's effort and focus even when things get rough.

Most adults have made commitments to work roles, family roles, religion, political ideology, and intimate relationships. These commitments reflect the priorities that a person believes give life meaning.

As an adult, you can appreciate the enormous complexity of addressing and resolving the issues of personal identity. You have discovered just how often you have relied on your sense of personal identity to make key life choices and to cope with the challenges of adulthood. The young person must weave together those elements of childhood identifications and personal history that continue to be valued, link them to a recognition of current talents and skills, and build commitments to the future. This creative synthesis brings a sense of wholeness, a solid base from which to venture forward into adulthood.

Having the advantage of experience, adults know that this sense of confidence and wholeness is not likely to be preserved throughout adulthood. After the initial crafting of personal identity, there are bound to be subsequent modifications, revisions, and extensions. But the vision of an integrated, meaningful person who stands for specific values, who has abilities of value to offer others, and who has the capacity to work hard to pursue goals—this first statement of a personal identity—is a powerfully invigorating achievement.

EXPLORING ROLES

To arrive at a personal synthesis, young people must feel free to explore a variety of roles. They begin to experiment with roles that appear to be attractive alternatives for the future. Role experimentation during college is similar to toddlers' and preschoolers' fantasy play. Pretending to be a fireman, a nurse, a mommy, or an astronaut gives young children a way to experience adult roles on a level that they can understand and control. They take bits and pieces of what they observe and put them together in a play sequence that makes sense to them. Play is not intended to be for real. The little boy who dresses up in a firefighter's outfit and goes about the room screeching like a fire truck does not really think he is a firefighter or a truck. He is just playing.

In some ways college students take the same attitude when they explore and experiment with roles. They may have various summer jobs, change college majors several times, go to services at different churches, date a variety of partners, experiment with unusual styles of dress, or campaign for political candidates from different parties. They may go through periods when they angrily reject many of your ideas and opinions. Then they return to ask for your advice and help with decisions. Unlike younger children who will usually tell you that they are only pretending, college students may play out roles as if they were for real. All of these behaviors are expressions of role experimentation.

Young people must try out different roles, ideas, and behaviors to see what fits. Many students also spend more time by themselves and, therefore, are able to recognize and reflect on their personal characteristics. Students need opportunities to discover as much about themselves as possible in order to resolve the questions that the search for personal identity poses. Parents sometimes become concerned because their son or daughter seems to be abandoning traditional family values in the process of role experimentation. The young person talks of changing his or her religion, remaining single, or selecting a low-status career. The more vehemently the family reacts, the more likely the young person is to become locked into a position in order to demonstrate autonomy.

Although it may be very difficult, parents need to remind themselves that much of their child's activities and ideas are still in an experimental phase. Children want to see how you react. The more you can retain a neutral stance, the more likely your child is to make good decisions—decisions that reflect his or her own real needs and values rather than ones that are tied into struggles for independence from parents. In the process, you gain some new freedom. You move out of the role of someone who lays down the rules and sets the agenda, and you become a partner with your child in thinking through tough choices.

EXPLORATION AND COMMITMENT

Work on identity formation requires two distinct components: exploration and commitment. First, young people need to question and experiment. This involves trying out new roles and new ideas to discover new possibilities and to determine which aspects of prior identifications still feel comfortable and authentic. Students need to learn as much as possible about the range and depth of their emotions, social skills, talents, interests, needs, and values. They need to encounter a diverse group of individuals who holds distinct values in order to determine what fits best with their own past, personal inclinations, and visions of the future. They also need to learn to examine complex situations in considering the implications of various choices and decisions for the expression of their personal values.

Often, this period of questioning and experimentation is accompanied by some uneasiness. It is like untying the moorings and drifting with the currents and the winds. Nothing is fixed, no single picture of oneself is clearly in focus. Young adults are on the edge of multiple images of the future; no single path appears more compelling or comfortable than the others. They may feel pressured by parents, peers, teachers, and others to make a choice, to decide on a course. The state of open questioning and experimentation is not one that our culture abides for long.

The second component is one of making commitments. After a time of questioning and examination, young people have to move toward some goals and away from others. They cannot walk along all paths at once. They may express their commitments by selecting a major, going steady, becoming engaged, joining a political party, becoming actively involved in a religious organization, or becoming involved in some form of community service. Personal identity is not only a product of examining alternatives but also of making choices and working hard to see those decisions through. In the process of making commitments, young people demonstrate for themselves and others how they have defined their personal meaning. They say, "This is how I wish to be known."

As parents, you need to be careful about assuming that commitments made during the college years are all equally permanent. One commitment may be held intensely, but for only six months. Another may be the beginning of a lifelong direction. In the early period of identity formation, it will not be easy to tell which commitments are going to last and which are temporary. Neither the young person nor the parents can be sure. Therefore, it is wise not to be overly enthusiastic about choices that you support or to worry too intensely about choices you think are wrong. It should be reassuring to appreciate that your child is giving a positive sign of development when he or she is able to experience a period of uncertainty or questioning and then to bring it to a close through the formation of a commitment.

DIFFERENT ORIENTATIONS TOWARD IDENTITY FORMATION

Young people come to college with different orientations toward personal identity. Four levels of identity can be described based on the two components—exploration and commitment. The levels are: having commitment without exploration, actively searching and questioning without commitment, having a personal identity in place, and being unable to achieve a personal identity.

Most adolescents arrive at college having made commitments without much exploration. Their values and goals are basically a product of their family and community cultures. They want for themselves what others have wanted for them. They have not experienced the uncertainty or the experimentation that is common during the college years. Thus, their commitments are based more on past identifications and family history than on a real understanding of their own characteristics. These young people usually revise their commitments as they experience the diversity of people, ideas, and activities that are part of university life.

For some students, however, the confrontation of their firm values and beliefs with choices and diversity can be troublesome. It may take some time for such students to recognize that it is all right, even positive, to have periods of doubt and confusion.

Many young people enter a period of active searching and questioning when they come to college. They are free of the daily expectations of their homes and high schools. These students view the college years as a time to experiment and explore. They have not yet made any commitments, and they do not feel any urgency about doing so. For these young people, college promises the freedom to try out different activities and roles and to visualize different versions of the self. Pressures from the adult world to establish an identity that can be known to others and a self that can be held accountable are temporarily suspended. One young woman describes a complete sense of openness as she approached the college years, an openness derived from a life in which very few options appeared to be available to women.

> When I went to college, I had no sense of direction, or even of myself. I majored in English because it was easy for me. I have always wanted to work with animals; in my family circle (sort of middle-class arty) women were either mothers or monsters. That is, there were only two choices—you conformed (wife/mother) or you didn't (beatnik/artist/

writer). I had never had what is called a "normal" life-
style—we heated with wood, had outdoor plumbing, ate
muskrat and raccoon and shellfish. It was very hard for me
to come to grips with middle-class society—I didn't understand any of the conventions and only some of the language. It really never occurred to me that anyone I knew
could become a doctor, lawyer, etc. Those options were not
part of my everyday life. We lived in the woods and [usu-
ally stayed there]. Nobody had careers! Or even jobs!
(*Bryn Mawr Alumni Bulletin*, 1981, p. 3)

Others—not many—arrive at college having given quite
a lot of thought to personal identity. Due to circumstances
of life, they have already faced a period of questioning and
experimentation that has freed them from heavy reliance
on past identifications. They have a pretty clear idea of
what they want for themselves, and they feel that their
choices are based on a high level of self-understanding.
Students who have been through certain kinds of life
crises, such as parental divorce or serious illness during
adolescence, may have done a lot of thinking along these
lines already. Students who have delayed coming to college
and have worked or traveled for a year or two probably
have made progress on personal identity issues before they
arrive. For most students, however, the process of achieving identity takes the better part of the four or five years of
college.

Two groups of students are unable to form a personal
identity during the college years. One group remains rig-
idly committed to the childhood vision of what they should
be. They are committed to values they learned and accepted from parents, teachers, religious leaders, friends,
peers, and others. These people are so strongly committed
during the college years that they fail to examine new

values or respond to newly emerging personal characteristics. In adult life, they lean heavily on the expectations of others to define their personal goals and commitments.

Students in the second group appear to lose their way amid the many alternatives and possibilities. These students cannot form a unified view of themselves. The possibility of making commitments creates intense anxiety. As they draw close to a commitment, the feeling of losing control or giving up a part of the self becomes so strong that they back away from the commitment.

We see an indication of this problem in some students who cannot resolve the decision to select a major. They choose a major for one or two quarters, then shift to something else for two quarters, and then go on to the next choice. These students cannot really make progress toward a degree because they cannot make the kinds of commitments that are required of adult life. This same kind of difficulty may be seen in their efforts to form intimate relationships. Once the possibility of closeness becomes a reality, they draw back. It is as if in getting close, they risk losing part of their self-concept.

The problem of being unable to achieve a personal identity becomes noticeable toward the end of the college years and in the period just following college. Before that time, during high school, most adolescents are in an exploratory state. The culture really does not demand the type of commitments that make the inability to form an identity show up as problematic for a high school student. However, as young people stand on the threshold of adulthood, the society exercises its influence. The college years do not last forever. Even if students go on to postgraduate education, thereby prolonging entry into the labor market, they are expected to select an area of expertise, make decisions about intimate relationships, and state value positions. Those students who remain confused and who are extremely fearful of commitments cannot move ahead and embrace the challenges of adulthood.

Faculty members, counselors, residence hall staff, and academic advisors are aware that some young people experience this anxiety about commitments. Most college campuses offer counseling and consultation services to help students work on identity-related problems. Residence hall advisors and faculty advisors who have interacted frequently with students may be able to tell the difference between a young person who is in a period of playful exploration and one who is anxiously avoiding any serious commitments. They can encourage such a student to seek help.

However, most people on campus will not interact with your child over a period of several years. As a parent, you must keep an eye open. By the junior or senior year, if you sense that your child is still treading water and unusually anxious, struggling to avoid making any decisions or commitments, you may want to urge your child to seek professional advice.

THE SIGNIFICANCE OF FORMING A PERSONAL IDENTITY

Successfully forming a personal identity results in a new sense of ownership over the direction of a young person's life course. It is the process of change, not the final decisions, that is of utmost importance. Two young people may arrive at very similar choices through quite distinct paths. A person's willingness to undergo a period of openness to alternatives and to examine personal values and goals critically is central to the formation of personal identity.

For example, one young man may arrive at college having decided to become an engineer. He was good in math in high school. He was encouraged by his parents and teachers to study engineering in college, and he selected engineering as a major when he entered college. He pursued the engineering curriculum, spent his time meeting the requirements of the program, and graduated with an engineering degree. He was pleased with his work at each step and was encouraged in his decisions by his parents and teachers. Some of his friends urged him to get involved with student government and other student activities, but he never felt he had the time or interest. He partied on the weekends and studied hard all week long.

This young man experienced commitment without experimentation. He never explored any alternatives and never questioned whether his decision fit his own temperament or talents. He never critically examined the implications of his decision for his future life-style or his personal values.

A second young man arrived at college undecided about a major. He spent his first year taking a variety of courses in math, science, and social science. He talked with his advisor, his parents, his friends, and did a lot of reading about career paths. During his sophomore year, he experienced a period of real frustration and worry about not having chosen a major. He gave some serious thought to business, economics, and computer science; but he never felt entirely confident about pursuing any of these fields.

During the summer following his sophomore year, he applied for a job as a research assistant in an engineering laboratory. He met some of the students and professors. He attended the brown bag lunch seminars that were held in the department. He found that he enjoyed the kinds of research activities and projects that the engineers were doing. He took a few engineering courses and some of the more advanced science courses that were required for an engineering major. He did well in the courses and continued to be interested in the approach to problem solving that was emphasized. By the middle of his junior year, he decided on engineering as a major. He completed the program and graduated with a degree in engineering.

The final outcome for these two young men may look very similar. Colleges and universities do not grant separate degrees for a Bachelor of Science in Engineering with full exploration and commitment and a Bachelor of Science in Engineering with commitment but no exploration. The difference in the two paths is in the greater sense of experimentation and questioning the second student experienced while reaching his decision.

The influence of this important difference in the process is not likely to be observed until some years later when both young men face the difficult and often ambiguous decisions of adult life. The young person who has undergone a period of uncertainty and questioning has gained practice in an important aspect of adult life. Most adult choices have more than one correct answer. Many possible futures exist. A challenge of adulthood is selecting the path that makes the greatest use of your talents and is also congruent with your interests, values, and goals. Having experienced the tensions and uncertainties in the decision to select a college major, a young person is much more adequately prepared to face the more difficult, complex decisions of a changing and unpredictable future.

In the process of forming a personal identity, everyone has temporary moments of confusion and depression. The task of bringing together the many elements of a person's experience into a coordinated, clear self-definition is difficult and time-consuming. You can expect your college-age child to go through periods of self-preoccupation, isolation, and discouragement as the diverse pieces of the identity puzzle are shifted and reordered into a total picture. Even the person who eventually achieves an integrated personal identity will experience some time when he or she despairs about life's meaning. Most young people make significant progress during the college years. They leave college more appreciative of the past, more confident about their abilities, and more genuinely inspired about being able to contribute meaningfully to their professions, their families, and their communities.

ADDITIONAL READING

Blos, P. (1962). *On adolescence: A psychoanalytic interpretation.* New York: The Free Press.

Erikson, E. H. (1950/1963). *Childhood and society.* New York: Norton.

———. (1968). *Identity: Youth and crisis.* New York: Norton.

———. (1982). *The life cycle complete: A review.* New York: Norton.

Kroger, J. (1989). *Identity in adolescence: The balance between self and other.* London: Routledge.

Whitbourne, S. K. (1986). *The me I know: A study of adult identity.* New York: Springer-Verlag.

Values

VALUES AND IDENTITY

The clarification of values is central to identity formation. The whole idea of making commitments requires an awareness of what you care about. During college, young people examine the principles, ideals, and achievements that give life meaning. They want to make a difference in this world, to believe that their lives are worthwhile. To achieve a sense of personal identity, a young person has to take a stand on some values and goals. To get to that point, most students go through a process of exploring different beliefs. They believe passionately in something for a while, and then six months later believe passionately in something quite different. The process of exploring and questioning values is similar to the process of identity formation in other areas such as gender-role and career choice.

It may be hard for adults to understand how students feel while they are in this process of value examination. As adults, most of us have already made commitments to certain values. Our family life, our work, and our reputation in the community reflect decisions that we made in our twenties and thirties to place certain ideals and goals ahead of others. After twenty years or more of commitment to values, it becomes difficult to remember what it was like to develop them. We do not usually examine our values on a day-to-day basis. Rather, we act upon them.

From time to time, however, life's challenges have a way of testing our values. We suddenly become aware of how important certain ideals and principles are to us when our ideals are called into question. Adults face many crises that force them to reexamine their values. This may occur when a loving relative dies before her time, a son or daughter becomes addicted to drugs, a marriage ends in divorce, a business falls into bankruptcy, a fire destroys prized possessions, or a nation faces a scandal in government. With each of these and similar crises, we are forced to confront and answer some of the following questions: What makes us feel worthwhile? What gives life meaning? How well do our actions and our decisions reflect our values? Do we live a life of integrity, or does a significant gap exist between what we say we believe and what we actually do from day to day? These are the kinds of thoughts and troubling feelings that accompany a review of values. The personal questioning that adults undergo in a crisis is very similar to the self-reflection that college students experience as they examine and commit to values.

Clarifying values is not simply an intellectual exercise. It involves more than reading different opinions and selecting the opinion that makes the most sense. It requires more consideration than weighing the costs and benefits of different positions and selecting the one with the most benefits. College students realize that their values can reach deeply into their lives, affecting their friendships, feelings about their parents, academic decisions, love relationships, and, at times, their personal safety. They begin to understand that a commitment to certain values may demand stressful courses of action, actions that may go against the tide of peer or parental opinion.

Think for a moment of the passion that college students have brought to the expression of social values in the past: the anti–Vietnam War protests, the civil rights movement, the women's liberation movement, protests against apartheid in South Africa, and nuclear disarmament. During college, students discover their voices, their ability to speak collectively about important social and political issues. They also discover some of the responsibilities, obligations, and risks that come along with taking a stand.

UNDERSTANDING STUDENTS' VALUES

The process of value development does not begin from scratch during the college years. Students arrive at college with a variety of values. They have some expectations about the directions their lives will take during college. Most students are ready to pursue some goals. A national survey of more than 200,000 students who entered as full-time college freshmen in the fall of 1989 describes the kinds of experiences and goals that are most important to them as they begin college (Astin, 1989).

Why do students attend college? They believe that a college education will enable them to achieve certain life goals. The most frequently endorsed reasons for going to college are to be able to get a better job, to learn more about things, and to make more money. Students see a close connection between a college degree and economic values. Students believe that the costs in time, money, and effort that are associated with completing a college degree are worthwhile because they bring economic security.

More than 50 percent of the students expect to continue on for a second degree. This kind of planning suggests that students have very ambitious career aspirations. It also suggests that they value the opportunities that additional education can provide. If you combine this agenda with the strong endorsement of coming to college in order to learn more, it is clear that students expect to develop some academic expertise. They place a strong value in acquiring knowledge that will help them function as an expert or an authority. We do not know if students expect to go on for another degree immediately, but we know that they see educational experiences as playing a continuing role in their adult lives.

Table 3.1 presents the reasons why it is very important to attend college and the percentage of more than 200,000 students surveyed who endorsed those reasons.

Table 3.2 shows some of the objectives students have as they begin college. These objectives are considered essential or very important in life. The three values that are most often rated as essential or very important are being very well-off financially, becoming an authority in one's field, and raising a family. Once again, you can see the reflection of two basic values, economic security and developing expert knowledge. The third value, raising a family, is one that is not associated with a decision to come to college. College freshmen do not yet appreciate how their college education will contribute to their ability to function effectively as marriage partners or as parents. However, those of us who work in colleges and universities are aware that much of the learning that takes place, both in the classroom and outside the classroom, can build skills that enhance family life.

Table 3.1
Reasons Noted as Very Important for Attending College

(PERCENTAGES)

Nothing better to do	2.4
Could not find a job	7.0
To get away from home	15.0
Parents wanted me to go	34.3
To become a more cultured person	35.6
To improve reading and study skills	40.5
To prepare for graduate school	51.5
To gain a general education	62.5
To be able to make more money	72.2
To learn more about things	72.4
To be able to get a better job	75.9

Source: Astin, A. W. (1989). *The American freshman: National norms for fall, 1989.* American Council on Education and University of California at Los Angeles.

The information in table 3.2 suggests that men and women have similar, but not identical, values as they begin college. Being very well-off financially is at the top of the list for men and women. Women express somewhat greater social concern than men in their more frequent endorsement of the objectives of helping others in difficulty and influencing social values. Men place somewhat greater emphasis than women on success in business, politics, and science. These values are characteristic of a slightly more conservative political position that young men take when compared to young women. About 29 percent of freshmen men describe themselves as politically conservative or to the far right ideologically. About 18 percent of freshmen women describe themselves that way.

Table 3.2

Life Objectives Considered Essential or Very Important

(PERCENTAGES)	MEN	WOMEN	TOTAL
Create artistic work	12	13	12
Be an authority in my field	68	64	66
Be successful in my own business	50	41	45
Be very well-off financially	79	72	75
Develop a philosophy of life	40	42	41
Have administrative responsibility	45	43	44
Help others in difficulty	49	69	60
Influence political structure	22	18	20
Influence social values	35	46	41
Keep up to date with politics	43	36	39
Obtain recognition from colleagues	56	54	55
Participate in community action	20	26	23
Promote racial understanding	32	38	35
Raise a family	68	69	69
Make theoretical contribution to science	21	14	17
Write original works	12	13	12

Source: Astin, A. W. (1989). *The American freshman: National norms for fall, 1989.* American Council on Education and University of California at Los Angeles.

The initial differences in values between young men and young women suggest that they may differ in what they hope to get out of college. Although the two groups share many common values, some aspects of a college environment might be of greater importance to male students and others may be of greater importance to female students. These differences may be expressed in their choice of a college; in their selection of a major; and in the way they become involved in the social, political, and intellectual life of the college community.

ENCOUNTERING VALUES
IN THE COLLEGE ENVIRONMENT

Starting with values and goals that were developed during childhood and adolescence, students encounter the value-laden environment of their college communities. Students have some ideas about why they want a college education and about what makes life meaningful. These ideas are expanded, revised, and reordered as a consequence of interactions with faculty, other students, visiting lecturers, books, films, music, theater, and the many other voices that contribute to the totality of a college education.

A college education gives students practice in assessing sources of information as well as in critically evaluating ideas. Students learn to distinguish the objective information from the values imbedded in the messages. Being exposed to many value positions through interaction with a wide range of scholars, disciplines, and theories gives students continuous opportunity to reflect upon and evaluate their own values. One goal of most introductory college courses is to help students differentiate statements of fact from statements of belief or opinion. Another goal is to help students recognize their own points of view and to appreciate the role that their own values and goals play in the way they interpret information. Value examination and development begins in the first days students arrive on campus and continues throughout their college careers.

As an educational institution, a college has a stake in promoting certain values that may or may not already be a part of each student's personal values. As you watch your child become more fully involved in the social and academic environment of college life, you will probably see some evidence of these values. Educational values include a commitment to the worth of ideas, freedom of inquiry and communication, the nurturing of innovation and creativity, respect for individuality and diversity, the promotion of competence and mastery as the bases for status, and a preference for reason and logic over intuition and faith as the bases for knowledge.

Review the list of essential life objectives presented in table 3.2. You might guess which ones are close to the hearts of most college faculty members. They are very likely to value making contributions to science, literature, and the arts. They are likely to value becoming an authority in one's field and receiving recognition from colleagues. Many college faculty members have achieved distinction as a result of original written works and creative accomplishments. Through their research and scholarly writings, they have contributed to the formation of social values, to shaping the political structure, and to addressing significant social problems.

Although college faculty members receive good salaries, you could not really say that most of them are very well-off financially. Almost 50 percent of the students who attend college have parents whose income is above that of an assistant professor at a university. Thus, college students are likely to encounter value conflicts as they come into contact with graduate students and faculty members who have chosen a life that reflects a very different economic value from the one to which they aspire. These encounters with diverse value positions are part of what stimulates a critical process of value examination.

PHASES IN THE DEVELOPMENT OF VALUES

Development of values typically occurs in four phases: knowing your values, questioning them, accepting others' values, and making value commitments (Perry, 1968). Students come to college having made different amounts of progress in establishing certain values and understanding the obligations that are linked to those commitments. The overall process leads to greater maturity and higher levels of ethical responsibility, but some points along the path may appear very much like backsliding. For this reason, it is important that you, as parents, understand the phases of value development and their contribution to a student's overall growth toward adulthood.

Knowing what you value

Students usually come to college feeling pretty confident about their beliefs and values. Often they come from a family and home community in which there is strong support for their family's values. Other families who live in the neighborhood, who attend their religious organization, and with whom they interact every day are likely to share many of the same basic life goals and social values. Studies of high-school-age adolescents and their parents find that adolescents are actually quite similar to their parents on most value issues, especially those related to religion, politics, and education. Thus, most students come to college thinking that they know what to value, that what they value is right, and that most of the other important people in their world value many of the same things they do.

Questioning what you value

The next phase in the development of values for students involves beginning to question what they value. This may occur as they confront value positions that are at odds with their own. The less experience students have had talking with people who have different goals and values, the less prepared they will be to defend their own value systems. Long conversations between roommates, intense discussions with instructors, or the burning indignation a student feels when an invited lecturer challenges his or her beliefs, all contribute to the initiation of a process of questioning. This is typically a very painful time for students. They are apt to feel confused, even angry, at finding so much room for alternatives in areas that they believed were correct.

Consider, as an example, the values about family life and the experiences of a female college freshman named Maureen. Maureen grew up believing that her adult life would bring marriage, childbearing, and parenting. She believed that her life would not be fulfilled without those experiences. In addition, she has placed such a high value on those goals that they have influenced other important decisions, including her career goals, her involvement with her community church, and her attitudes toward the boys she dated in high school.

Upon coming to college, Maureen becomes aware that there is quite a lot of controversy about the value of family life. In conversations with roommates and other young women in the dorm, she learns that several of her friends are thinking about remaining single. She takes a course in sociology in which a variety of family forms is discussed and analyzed. She attends a lecture about the "mommy track" in business, in which the speaker argues that career women who have children should not be expected to compete with single or childless women or with men. She begins dating a boy who says his ideal life is to be married to a career woman who would be just as independent and self-sufficient as he plans to be.

All of these experiences introduce uncertainty for Maureen. Values and goals that she had accepted without question are now open to examination. She realizes that her views are not shared universally. She also realizes that consequences and responsibilities are attached to her family values. Maureen is faced with the difficult challenge of reexamining some very basic assumptions that have given structure to her self-concept and to her view of the future.

Now that she is aware of the alternatives, Maureen will begin a process of critical examination and reflection about the commitments she is making. As a result, Maureen will likely emerge with a stronger, more deeply held set of values that will be more resilient in the face of opposing views and challenges. Her values may or may not be modified in the process, but they will reflect a greater understanding of her own needs as well as a greater sense of personal obligation and commitment to the values she eventually embraces.

Accepting all value positions as reasonable

The third phase of value development is a period of total value relativism or flexibility. This position was expressed in the 1960s by the saying "different strokes for different folks," in the 1970s by the expression "do your own thing," and in the 1980s by the advice to "chill out" or "lighten up." It refers to the philosophy that no one can say what is right or best for someone else. Each person has a right to his or her own values. Almost any values can make sense if they are examined from the point of view of the person who cherishes them. From that perspective, no values are more acceptable or worthy than any others. You would not reject a person because he or she had different values, nor would you take the responsibility to try to influence the beliefs of someone whose values were different from your own.

You can understand from the example of Maureen how such an attitude toward values can develop within the college environment. The combination of different voices, the pressure to take an objective stance toward information, and the desire to fit into an intense social environment, are all forces that support suspending judgment. Students learn not to judge each other too quickly but to remain open to the many arguments and opinions voiced by their peers. In the classroom, students are often surprised to read evidence that contradicts commonly held beliefs and opinions. They become aware of convincing points of view they did not know existed. The development of new levels of critical reasoning requires that students suspend judgment while they explore different sources of information and opposing theories. Students discover that they are in a better position to cope with the social and the intellectual demands of college life if they can remain open to different ideas and avoid rejecting new views.

As parents, you may find this phase of your child's value exploration most frustrating. You were probably quite proud of your child's many accomplishments during high school, and you may have believed that you had achieved some basic agreement about the goals that were worth pursuing. Suddenly, you find your child stating value positions or defending views that seem quite distant from your own. You may hear discussions that suggest that material achievements are much more important, or much less important, than you believe them to be. College students may become involved in exploring a range of spiritual and religious beliefs and practices that are foreign to you. Your son or daughter may participate in political clubs, rallies, or campaigns that support issues you oppose.

What is even more difficult, if you challenge these activities, your child may respond by saying that he or she respects your right to believe as you do, and that you should do likewise. In other words, you may not even get a fight. Instead, you may get a rather condescending response that conveys disappointment that you are too "hung up" on your values, and that you ought to try to be more free-thinking. Of course, it is natural to be "hung up" on values that have been guiding your decisions for twenty years or more. And it is just as natural to be freethinking within the supportive environment of the college community.

It is important to view this phase of value exploration as a kind of experimentation. If you can recognize this phase as part of a larger, prolonged process of establishing enduring commitments, you will be less likely to overreact to any single one of these ventures into new value directions.

Making value commitments

The final phase in value development involves making personal commitments. This takes time and occurs in different value areas at different points. Work-related values are likely to be established early, since there is pressure to decide on a major and to select a career path. Political and social values take shape as students become integrated into the social life of college. These areas demand significant and repeated value commitments. Students find themselves needing to make decisions as voters, as friends, as intimate companions, and as members of the community.

Religious values are likely to be slow in developing since most colleges and universities give them very little attention. Students are left to pursue these questions on their own or as members of religious communities.

Through the process of identification, students' values are shaped by the values of people in leadership roles. One aspect of making value commitments involves the desire to feel connected to other students, teachers, advisors, or campus leaders who express clear value positions. Students meet people on campus who are very clear about their values and who try to encourage others to work along with them. These people may be organizing a volunteer program for low-income youths in the community; they may be planning a study tour to China; they may be establishing an investment club for students; or they may be the leaders of the Young Democrats, the Young Republicans, or the Socialist party on campus.

Another component of making value commitments is fostered as students become more confident about the kind of futures they desire. As a young adult falls in love and begins to imagine a future with a loving companion, the goals and values of that person become relevant in shaping the young adult's own values. As students develop close friendships, they are influenced by wanting to share the values and retain the respect and support of their friends. Their commitment to certain values may be an expression of friendship. As students gain confidence about the discipline in which they are majoring, their value commitments reflect those of the discipline and those that students believe they can contribute through their discipline to the larger society.

VALUE DIFFERENCES BETWEEN PARENTS AND THEIR COLLEGE STUDENTS

By and large, the value differences between students and their parents are not that great. The more children perceive their parents as reasonable and understanding, the more they tend to identify with their parents' values and goals. As parents involve their children in family decisions and turn to them for advice, children have an opportunity to contribute to the attainment of family goals. In this process, the children become invested in those goals as well.

Of course, some differences in values between college students and their parents will emerge. Students tend to overestimate the differences, seeing themselves as more distinct from their parents than they really are. Parents of college students tend to underestimate the differences, seeing their children as more similar to them than they really are.

Parents and children each have a somewhat different stake in this process. Parents, who are in the middle of their adult years, are living out the consequences of value commitments they made in their twenties and thirties. Certainly, they will have time to reevaluate and modify their commitments for the future. Nonetheless, parents have a stake in wanting to demonstrate that the decisions they have made have led to productive, meaningful lives for themselves and a good start on life for their children.

College students have their individuality and their autonomy at stake. It is important for them to perceive that they are making decisions on their own, that they are in control of their future. What is more, they are trying to achieve a comfortable psychological distance from their parents by emphasizing those areas where their commitments are different. They are at a natural time to examine their values as they prepare to make the commitments they will follow.

Your view of the important objectives of adult life was influenced by the norms of life as you faced them twenty or thirty years ago. Although you might consider some of your own values to be essential for any ethical person regardless of the historical era, other values change as society changes. New career opportunities, possibilities for new international collaborations, remarkable technological innovations, and dramatic changes in the acceptance of diverse life-styles are only a few examples of societal changes that affect your child's outlook on his or her emerging adulthood.

What is more, your child is far more aware of the likelihood of change in the society than you were at the same age. Books and magazine articles address issues of information overload and information management, how to plan for a changing future, and how to cope with the stresses of an uncertain and changing world. Your child's values are taking shape within this context. It makes sense to assume that some of your child's value commitments reflect an adaptation to the demands as well as the opportunities of a rapidly changing culture.

Value examination and value commitment are of basic importance to the process of identity formation. By the end of the college years, young people must begin to understand which goals they care about and are willing to work for. Values are the guidelines that help people operate in difficult situations. Students must begin to take responsibility for the consequences of their commitments, especially in the face of opposing pressures and temptations to abandon their values. Without this type of value commitment, students will be awash in a sea of alternatives. They must achieve the courage and the competence to take actions that reflect their values as they make the early critical decisions of their adult lives.

ADDITIONAL READING

Astin, A. W. (1977). *Four critical years: Effects of college on beliefs, attitudes, and knowledge.* San Francisco: Jossey-Bass.

Clemenza, R. (1990). *Four years: Knucklehead's guide to college life.* Midland Park, NJ: Knuthouse.

Gilligan, C. (1982). *In a different voice: Psychological theory and women's development.* Cambridge, MA: Harvard University Press.

Perry, W. G., Jr. (1968). *Forms of intellectual and ethical development in the college years.* New York: Holt, Rinehart and Winston.

4 | College Communities

There are currently more than 3,200 institutions of higher education in the United States, including universities, their branch campuses, four-year colleges, and two-year colleges. Colleges have become major educational and socialization settings for American youth. Young people may enroll in postsecondary education because of parental expectations, peer pressure, career aspirations, the lack of job opportunities for high school graduates, and a search for new ideas and new information. In the 1980s completing a college degree brought a substantial economic advantage. The demand for college-educated employees has exceeded the supply, and this pattern is projected to continue throughout the 1990s (Murphy and Welch, 1989). For all these reasons, more than seven million young people in the age range eighteen to twenty-four attend these complex educational institutions each year.

Students enter college in pursuit of their own educational and occupational goals. They will be touched by the mission, value orientation, and expectations of their new environment. College students experience demands for more logical reasoning, new levels of scholarship, community involvement, and friendship that can influence their intellectual, social, and emotional development throughout adulthood.

It is not uncommon to talk to adults who say that they learned how to think for themselves in college or that they learned the real value of friendship in college. During college, students are introduced to new standards of excellence, new levels of competition, new demands for hard work, and new opportunities for intellectual growth. These new challenges stand out in their minds, inspiring them toward higher levels of personal achievement.

Just so you do not think that all of college life is a great and wonderful search after ideas and insights, we should call up some of the less idealistic images as well. Students gripe and groan about their professors, they fall asleep over their books, and they waste incredible amounts of time deciding how to avoid work. Students try to protect themselves from the overwhelming flood of information that persistently reminds them of their own relative ignorance. Often, they step cautiously from course to course, from friend to friend, trying to hold onto the threads of purpose and self-definition that started them on their journeys. As they move along, however, the voyage itself transforms their intentions so that by the end they have a new view of themselves. They seek new goals, impose new standards on themselves, and work hard to try to make things turn out the way they want them to.

KINDS OF COLLEGE EXPERIENCES AND THEIR IMPACT

The large number and different types of postsecondary institutions have a range of institutional missions. Colleges have their distinct advantages and disadvantages, their own particular climates. It is important to be aware of the characteristics of the college that can affect the quality of the students' experiences. Some of the obvious differences among colleges include:

the size of the student body
the cost of tuition
a two-year college or technical institute versus a
    bachelor's degree-granting institution
an undergraduate college versus a university
a public or private institution
a coeducational or a single-sex institution
a commuter campus that does not provide residence
    halls on the campus or a residential campus where
    most students live in dormitories or apartments
a historically black institution, a predominantly
    white institution, or an institution with
    substantial racial and ethnic diversity
an institution with a stated religious orientation or a
    nonsectarian college

These features will influence the campus atmosphere. They will have some impact on the variety of students who are enrolled, the nature of the students' outlook on their education, the goals of the faculty and the quality of their interactions with students.

The mission and characteristics of the college influence the priorities faculty have for the use of their time as well as the quantity and quality of services available to meet students' needs. Faculty at large research universities, for example, are expected to contribute significantly to the advancement of knowledge in their fields through research and other scholarly activities. They must balance the time they devote to teaching and advising students with time for research, writing, and presenting papers at professional meetings. These faculty usually teach at both the graduate and undergraduate levels. The faculty at research universities have to spend time keeping up to date with the latest developments in their fields so they can continue to be productive in teaching and research. These faculty are often called on to serve in advisory and consulting roles because of their academic specialty. Service to the community and to their professional associations is expected.

Students at large research universities have the benefit of attending classes and lectures given by leading scholars. They work in laboratories equipped with the most modern technology. They have access to a wide range of library and computer resources that support the teaching and the research missions of the university. Students begin to interact with graduate students who have made a commitment to advanced study in their fields. Students may have opportunities to become involved in research and to participate in pioneering programs that are part of their professors' scholarly work.

Undergraduate students at these universities may not have much personal contact with professors, especially during the first and second years. In the introductory courses, the lectures may be given by faculty, but the discussion sections or laboratories are often taught by graduate assistants. Students tend to feel somewhat anonymous with respect to their academic identities during their first year or two, until they begin to take the more advanced and specialized courses in their majors.

Faculty at four-year undergraduate colleges may continue to produce scholarly work and to publish, but their primary emphases are teaching, student advising, and working with students on independent projects and special assignments. These faculty are not usually responsible for graduate or professional students. They are expected to provide quality classroom instruction and to promote the intellectual growth of their students.

Since the expectations to conduct research are not as great at these institutions, there are fewer resources available for research. Thus, it is more difficult for the faculty to remain familiar with the newest technologies and innovations in their fields. However, they can provide a scholarly environment to foster students' enthusiasm and involvement in the learning process. Many of the students who decide to go on for graduate study and who pursue doctoral study at major research universities complete their undergraduate education at smaller liberal arts colleges where they develop a deep commitment to their discipline.

Students need to be adequately informed about the significant characteristics of a college before enrolling. Some colleges work harder than others to give prospective students a good glimpse of the college environment. Generally, the college bulletins and other written recruitment materials provide only a very limited view. Students need to visit the campus, stay in a residence hall, attend some classes, and get a sense of the resources available both on and off campus that will be important for meeting their personal as well as their academic needs.

It is difficult to evaluate any college setting as an outsider. However, you want to encourage your child to consider his or her own needs and goals as well as the strengths and weaknesses of the college setting before making a decision. Many times the trip to the campus is a good way to tell if your son or daughter feels comfortable or ill at ease. In addition, it is important to determine whether your child's academic and social needs are likely to be met by the environment of the college he or she has in mind. The better the initial fit between the student and the college, the more likely it is that the college environment will make an optimal contribution to the student's intellectual and personal growth.

ADAPTATION TO COLLEGE RESIDENCES

One of the more challenging experiences of college life is living in the residence halls. Most residential campuses require freshmen to spend their first year in a dormitory. Some colleges require students to remain in residence halls even longer. Think a moment about this experience. Young people from different family groups, different neighborhoods, different parts of the country, different racial and religious backgrounds, and even different countries are brought together to share bedrooms, bathrooms, hallways, laundry rooms, dining halls, and study areas. Young people, many of whom have never had to share a bedroom, converge into a relatively crowded living space. They have to coordinate their daily living patterns with many other students at a time when they are focusing intensely on their independence.

Life in the residence halls brings students face-to-face with hundreds of decisions they may never have made before. Students have to ask each other to hold down the noise, to take shorter showers, or to make shorter phone calls. Students depend on one another to take phone messages, to find another room for a night or two if a guest is visiting, and to share toothpaste or shaving cream in an emergency.

Amid the stresses of course work, exams, papers, athletic competition, conflicts with parents, faltering love relationships, and confusion about future aspirations, dormitory residents come to share one another's crises and triumphs. The nervous laughter or tears about a broken date, the screams and shouts of triumph over an A paper or a big football victory, and the crash of wastebaskets and aluminum cans during a weekend celebration are part of a dormitory's atmosphere. Some students love this environment and feel wonderful as they are drawn into its energetic confusion. Other students resent the intrusions into their privacy and feel that living in a dorm is an affront to their personal dignity.

The impact of residence halls on students' adjustment to college depends in part on architectural design and in part on social atmosphere. The design of the building, its upkeep, and the number of students who are living in one area all influence how it feels to live there. Freshmen are likely to form their earliest college friendships with the students who live in their dorm. The frequent conversations among roommates or suitemates contribute to the formation of friendships that may remain important throughout college.

The physical organization of the dormitory affects the quality of relationships that are formed (Baum and Valins, 1977; Null, 1980, 1981). When students live in a dormitory that is built around a long corridor with rooms on either side, the quality of contacts with other students seems to be impersonal. Students run into other students in the hallways, but they may not know each other; and they may not feel comfortable about these chance meetings. Students who live in this type of arrangement are likely to feel that the dorm is crowded and that they do not know their neighbors.

Dormitories that are organized into suites of two to four rooms off a central living space seem to encourage more positive social relationships. Students have a better opportunity to predict and control the frequency of contacts with other students. They can decide together how they will use their shared living space. The group of four to sixteen students whose rooms are joined form a base for social contact. These students not only get to know one another, but they link each other to a wider social network through other friendships on campus.

Residence halls also differ in their social climates. Some halls are known for their academic emphasis, while others have a reputation for creativity, socializing, tradition, or student involvement. The social atmosphere of university residence halls can be described along ten dimensions. The ten dimensions are grouped under four general categories: interpersonal relationships, personal growth, intellectual growth, and system change and maintenance (Gerst and Moos, 1972).

INTERPERSONAL RELATIONSHIPS: The emphasis on interpersonal relationships in the house.

1 . Involvement—the degree of commitment to the house and the residents; the amount of social interaction and feelings of friendship in the house.

2 . Emotional support—the extent of open concern for others in the house; efforts to help one another with academic and personal problems; emphasis on open and honest communication.

PERSONAL GROWTH: Social pressure related to specific dimensions of psychosocial development of the residents.

3 . Independence—the diversity of residents' behaviors that is allowed without social sanctions versus socially proper and conformist behavior.

4 . Traditional social orientation—the stress on dating, going to parties, and other traditional heterosexual activities.

5. Competition—the degree to which a wide variety of activities, such as dating and grades, is cast into a competitive framework.

INTELLECTUAL GROWTH: The emphasis placed on academic and intellectual activities related to the cognitive development of residents.

6. Academic achievement—the extent to which strictly classroom accomplishments and concerns are prominent in the house.

7. Intellectuality—the emphasis placed on cultural, artistic, and other intellectual activities, as distinguished from strictly classroom achievement.

SYSTEM CHANGE AND MAINTENANCE: The degree of stability versus the possibility for change in the atmosphere of the house.

8. Order and organization—the amount of formal structure or organization (e.g., rules, schedules, and established procedures), neatness.

9. Innovation—organizational and individual spontaneity of behavior and ideas, the number and variety of activities, new activities.

10. Student influence—the extent to which student residents (not staff or administrators) perceive that they control the running of the house; formulate and enforce the rules; control the use of the budget; select staff, food, and roommates; or make policies.

Many colleges and universities are sensitive to the different personal, social, and intellectual needs of their entering students. They have created specialized residence halls where the atmosphere is intended to meet the needs of certain groups of students. There may be houses or wings of residence halls for students who are in the honors program. Some colleges have language houses where all students speak German, Spanish, French, or some other language. Some universities have residence halls or floors for students who are studying a particular subject, such as home economics or engineering. This type of living arrangement gives students a chance to build social networks within their majors and to give one another support in managing the demands of their academic programs.

Coed dormitories are another housing innovation. In contrast to what you might expect, they tend to place a greater emphasis on intellectual life. They involve students in more cultural, artistic, and other intellectual activities than either all-male or all-female dorms. Students rate them as less competitive than all-male dorms and less social than all-female dorms. All three types of housing are similar in student involvement and influence and similar in concern about academic achievement in the classroom.

Recognizing the different atmospheres does not solve the question of how to select the best living arrangement for an individual student. In fact, most entering freshmen do not see dormitory life as the preferred form of housing, even in their freshmen year. Only 42 percent of the 1988 entering freshmen said that they preferred to live in the dormitories. However, 72 percent were actually planning to live in dormitories during the first quarter or semester of their freshman year (American Council on Education, 1988).

The dormitory experience has been a target of frequent criticism from both students and parents. Students complain about the noise and the difficulty of getting any studying done in the dorms. They complain about the food. And some students complain about the inability to exercise control over the disruptive behaviors of other students. Students have to be prepared to assert themselves when they believe that other students are overstepping the boundaries of decency or are taking unfair advantage of them. Most student life professionals endorse the philosophy that students need to learn to actively solve the problems they face in their living arrangements. There are both formal and informal procedures for resolving differences between roommates or the residents on the floor. The residence hall staff will try to encourage students to use their own negotiation and problem-solving skills to arrive at an acceptable solution. They may try to coach a student about how to approach the problem but will not step in to settle the problem themselves.

Sometimes students turn to their parents for help in resolving interpersonal problems. It is natural for parents to want to step in to defend their children and protect them from indignities or exploitation. However, it is important to listen carefully and determine whether your child has exhausted all the avenues available for resolving the problem on his or her own. At the same time, some problems are beyond a student's capacity to resolve. A roommate who is suicidal, harassment from racist students, or thefts in the residence hall are examples of issues that may lead parents to conclude that the student must find another place to live. You should expect the college staff to work with your student and you in resolving these and similar, serious problems in a student's living arrangements.

Parents may be worried by the poor quality of some of the living arrangements. Many of the residence halls are very old. The rooms are often small, dimly lit, and poorly ventilated. The level of cleanliness ranges from acceptable to terrible. Parents will find that most residence halls are far from luxurious, even when they are paying quite a lot of money for college tuition and dormitory fees.

Nevertheless, living in a residence hall clearly contributes to a student's ability to cope with college life. The residential experience is consistently identified among the factors that account for students staying in school and graduating. Students who live in the residence halls are more involved in campus life than are commuter students. Information about campus life, about special opportunities for students, and about issues facing students are transmitted in the most orderly way to the students who live in dorms. Students living in the residence halls get to know other students who may be quite unlike them. They encounter and struggle with varying points of view, values, and styles of resolving conflicts. Through peers as well as residence hall advisors and floor counselors, the residence halls provide sources of emotional and social support during times of significant personal and intellectual confusion.

The choice of a residence hall is probably not the most important factor in selecting a college or university. It certainly is not more important than the quality of the faculty, the quality of the courses offered in a student's area of interest, or the quality and diversity of the other students who attend the college. If choices are available to students, however, it does make sense for them to try to become familiar with the living arrangements that are possible and to select one or two that would best match their social and intellectual needs. Most colleges try to take these preferences into account when making dormitory assignments.

IDENTITY FORMATION AND THE COLLEGE EXPERIENCE

The amount of influence the college experience has on personal growth and identity formation depends on three factors: 1) the identity status of the student as he or she enters college, 2) the match between the value orientation of the college and the value orientation of the student, and 3) the amount and quality of student-faculty interaction.

The college's ability to influence the identity formation and value consolidation of students depends, in part, on the identity status of the individual student. As outlined in chapter 2, some students have made commitments to values and goals without much exploration.

A second group of students enters an active period of value exploration and experimentation when they come to college. They question their goals and values and try out different versions or images of themselves.

The third group of students finds it difficult, if not impossible, to make any firm commitments. They are unable to integrate the many roles they play into a consistent view of the self, and their inability to make commitments begins to be viewed as a problem during this time.

It is unlikely that many students enter college having achieved a sense of personal identity. As we mentioned earlier, some students who have experienced significant life challenges during the adolescent years may have done more questioning and examination of values than those who have experienced a more typical adolescence.

Students whose minds are already made up are less likely to change their values due to the influence of the college culture than are students who are questioning and exploring. For them the choice of college, the selection of a major, and decisions to participate in college activities are directed by a set of values and goals that have already been established. The college culture will either support that value system or disrupt it depending on the degree of fit between the student's values and those of the college.

If these students select a college that mirrors their own

value system, regardless of the amount of interaction between them and the faculty, this value system is likely to go
unchallenged. If they select a college that is at odds with
their value system or where they encounter a great diversity of values, change is more likely. The amount of change
depends on the amount of faculty-student interaction and
the extent to which students are encouraged and supported to explore their values.

If student-faculty interaction is frequent and the value
climate is quite different from that of the student, the
student is going to experience strong pressures to examine
his or her views. Some students become very uncomfortable with this pressure. They may not want to open themselves up to a process of value exploration. They may feel so
alienated from the environment that they decide to transfer to another school. Other students begin a process of
self-examination and exploration. They begin to engage
the issues and questions that are raised in the setting and
undergo the kind of critical questioning that eventually
leads to identity achievement. These students experience a
very powerful transformation during the college years that
is directly influenced by the college environment.

Students who are experiencing a lot of questioning and
exploring and who are in a college where faculty-student
contacts are infrequent will experience value change as a
product of role experimentation, logical thought about
value issues, interactions with their peers, and the gradual
integration of cultural, historical, and family values. The
college culture itself will make little contribution to the
student's identity formation. However, in environments
where more interaction takes place, these students will be
engaged in a dialogue with faculty and other students
about the values and goals that are important to the college community. Conversations that focus on value issues

generally evoke college students' interest because the students are developmentally sensitive to issues of value clarification. A college culture that promotes frequent interactions between students and faculty becomes a setting for student socialization and plays an influential role in the development of the students' values.

Students in these settings are likely to identify with and develop a strong sense of allegiance to the values of their college. They will feel a bond of common commitment with other students in their class who have struggled through these questions with them. Camaraderie develops among all students who have graduated from the institution. Students from these institutions understand and empathize with each other after having participated in a common socialization process.

IDENTITY CRISIS

The term *identity crisis* refers to a sudden disintegration or deterioration of the framework of values and goals that a person relies on to give meaning and purpose to daily life. Usually an identity crisis involves strong feelings of anxiety and depression. The anxiety occurs because the person fears that, without the structure of a clear value system, unacceptable impulses will break through and the person will behave in ways that might be harmful or immoral. The depression occurs because the person suddenly feels worthless. When previously established goals are viewed as meaningless, the person is likely to be overwhelmed by feelings that his or her actions have no purpose or value to himself or herself or to others.

Identity crises for college students may result from two different situations, both of which place demands for rapid, intense examination of value issues. First, identity crises may occur for students who attend a college that departs significantly from their own value orientation and where there is frequent faculty-student interaction. In this case, the students realize that the people with whom they have frequent interactions and with whom they are supposed to identify have values that are quite different from their own. These students suddenly feel at a loss when significant adults challenge their values. They believe they should admire and respect adults, especially professors. Yet they may try desperately to sustain their old value system in order to protect a sense of control.

This kind of conflict can occur when students who have very traditional values and clear career agendas attend highly selective and prestigious private colleges. Students may want to attend a college like Harvard or Stanford because of the status and reputation of the college. However, the students may be totally unprepared for the strong socialization pressures and norms for academic achievement in these and similar colleges. They may not anticipate the way they will respond to expectations to examine ideas objectively, to open themselves up to new views, and to experiment with many roles. Going to a prestigious liberal arts college is not the same as buying a Mercedes Benz or a Brooks Brothers suit. It is more than a status symbol; it is a life experience that can create intense conflict for students who are not prepared for it.

Thomas Cottle (1977) described the disorientation of a student who encountered academic failure for the first time when he came to college.

> "I don't know anything other than that I had a tremendous high school record. After that it seems like time stops. I'm like an . . . one of those guys who can't remember any-

thing. . . . I'm the amnesiac. The last two years? Nothing.
Absolutely nothing. Zero, man." He shrugged his shoul-
ders. "I *am* the zero man. Nothing good has gone into my
head and stayed there. Sixteen half courses and I couldn't
give you a paragraph about one of them. Not a word, man,
I couldn't even tell you what I studied the last two weeks
before finals." . . . He poked his finger against his temple.
"There's nothing up there, man. Not a damn thing but
sawdust and some high school chemistry." (p. 127)

Identity crises may also occur for students who are exploring and experimenting if external demands force them
to make a value commitment while they are still uncertain
or confused. For some students, the need to make a decision about selecting a major, to make a commitment to a
love relationship, or to take a stand on a campus controversy will convince them they do indeed know what they
want. They will be reassured to find that their values are
more fully shaped than they had realized. If this happens,
the student will move in the direction of identity achievement. For other students, however, the demands for commitment may throw them into even greater confusion. If
a student is profoundly uncertain about which values
and goals are best, sudden demands for commitment may
threaten to overwhelm the student and send the existing,
tentative value structure into disorganization.

As parents, you will be trying to read all the signals to
determine whether your child is coping well with the
college environment. You want to try to assess whether the
environment is challenging enough without being overwhelming. You want to try to understand whether your
child is able to cope with the social as well as the intellectual demands of the setting. In particular, you want to try
to assess the amount of conflict your child is experiencing

within the value climate of the college and whether that conflict appears to be growth promoting or disorienting.

We know that it is common for students to struggle with college life and to go through a period when they wonder if college in general or the specific college they are attending is really for them. However, it may be very difficult for you to know whether your child is having trouble adjusting to college. The following excerpt from a letter gives you a look at why one student is reluctant to share his confusion with his parents:

> I am not telling my parents that I don't really want to be here. They think that I love it here. I don't know why I don't want to be here. I have a lot of friends and better-than-average grades. I just feel like I should be doing something else, but I don't know what. It's all so confusing.
>
> I have never told my parents this because they appear to be very happy with what I am doing, and I don't want to spoil it for them.

Some students believe they must convince their parents that college is just wonderful. They believe that their parents are making significant sacrifices to send them to college, and they want their parents to think that the college experience is everything they had hoped for.

Some students are ashamed that they are not happy. They feel that they would be disappointing their parents if they admitted that they were having difficulties fitting into the college culture or that they felt too confused to make the kinds of choices and decisions that a college program requires.

Some students may be attending the college that their parents attended. They fear that any expression of disappointment about this college may be taken as a personal rejection of their parents' choice.

Many students who have been looking forward to going to college find that they are more homesick and lonesome for their family and hometown friends than they had expected. They are embarrassed to admit that it is not quite as wonderful to be on their own as they had hoped.

For these and many other reasons, you may have to be a skillful sleuth to detect whether your son or daughter has made the right choice of a college and whether your child is adjusting well to the demands of college life. It may help to let your child know that you are aware that the first few months, even the first year, of college can be very rough. This will allow your child to express his or her reservations and concerns more openly.

You will need to keep attuned to unusual signs of stress, especially vulnerability to illness, unusual tiredness, sleeplessness, dramatic shifts in mood, unusual changes in appetite—either loss of appetite or overeating—and increased complaints about back pain, headaches, nausea, or other physical symptoms. These and other symptoms of stress are an indication that the demands of the situation are pushing the student to the limit. Try not to be overly enthusiastic about your child's allegiance to the college he or she has chosen, and keep the door open to the possibility of a change.

Most students really do thrive at college. They select a school that complements their abilities and goals, and they take pride and pleasure in their new levels of achievement. You would not want to make the mistake of interpreting expressions of pleasure and satisfaction as a cover-up for problems. On the other hand, it should not come as a complete surprise to you if you learn that your child has decided to transfer to another school or to drop out of school for a while. College environments differ, students differ, and the match between the two simply does not always work out well for everyone.

ADDITIONAL READING

Astin, A. W., Green, K. C., and Korn, W. S. (1987). *The American freshman: Twenty year trends, 1966–1985.* Los Angeles: The Higher Education Research Institute of UCLA.

The Chronicle of Higher Education. A weekly publication that focuses on issues, trends, and concerns regarding postsecondary education.

Cottle, T. J. (1977). *College: Reward and betrayal.* Chicago: University of Chicago Press.

Jeakle, B. and Wyatt, E. (1989). *How to college in the 90s.* New York: New American Library, Penguin Books.

Kaye, E. and Gardner, J. (1988). *College bound: The students' handbook for getting ready, moving in, and succeeding on campus.* New York: The College Entrance Examination Board.

Lockerbie, D. B. and Fonesca, D. R. (1990). *College: Getting in and staying in.* Grand Rapids, MI: William B. Eerdmans.

Rosovksy, H. (1990). *The university: An owner's manual.* New York: Norton.

 Friendship and
Loneliness

*F*riends play a key role in promoting your well-being. Your friends provide social support, they help you feel valued and important, and they share information and resources. In times of crisis, they can step in to help relieve some of your difficulties. Friends can contribute to your successes and join in your celebrations.

Although friends are important throughout life, they play a somewhat different role at different ages. College students need to find friends who understand the fundamental questions they are raising and who will help them continue to make progress in clarifying their identity. Young adults become less conforming and more independent in their judgments during the college years. They are less likely to seek peer friendships in order to be accepted by a clique or crowd. They are more interested in honesty and commitment in friendships. As college students try to understand their own personal qualities, talents, and goals, they need to find friends who can help them clarify these issues. Through conversations, questioning, and shared experiences, college friends help one another recognize and value personal qualities and develop a shared vision of the future.

The following letter was written by a college student in response to a request to describe some aspect of college life that he normally would not discuss with his parents. The letter reflects the important role that friendship plays as a component of the college experience. The letter writer also points out that parents may not find out very much about their child's social life at college or about the friendships their children are forming.

> Mostly, what I don't tell my parents deals with my social life, although I see that as the biggest learning experience at State. The parties and various activities which go on down here with other people would seem to detract from my studying, but I see it as more of a help than a hindrance. The dorms are a great place since there are so many people and late nights seem to bring out the conversationalists in all of us.

Against a backdrop of students from different family experiences, geographic areas, races, religions, talents, and goals, each college student has the opportunity to begin to clarify his or her unique characteristics. As they make friends, students begin to understand themselves more clearly and they find kindred spirits.

THE DEVELOPMENT OF FRIENDSHIP

The quality of friendship changes from high school through the college years. College students become more selective in their choice of friends. They become more understanding of other people's points of view. Because of this, they can be more effective in meeting their friends' needs. Friendships become more reciprocal, friends tend to do things for each other and take vicarious pleasure from each other's successes.

One of Jack Kennedy's best friends throughout his life was LeMoyne (Lem) Billings, a friend he made at the Choate School.

> "Jack was always trying to test Lem by entering him into competition, almost as his second. . . . Both of them got, I think, vicarious satisfaction out of each other's achievements. They were able to get as much pleasure out of the other person's success as they did out of their own. Later on, Lem certainly enjoyed Jack's political successes as much as Jack Kennedy did. And I think that Jack probably enjoyed it when Lem won a wrestling match as much as Lem enjoyed it. He enjoyed Lem's strength and physical abilities probably even more than Lem because Lem never really put that much stock in his own enormous strength. It was almost as if all the times Lem demonstrated his physical prowess he did it for Jack as a return, as part of a sort of reciprocal arrangement in which each of them would show off the best of their abilities so that the other one could take enjoyment out of something that he couldn't do himself." (Michaelis, 1983, p. 158, quoted from Robert Kennedy, Jr.)

During college, friends experience greater depth in understanding each other's feelings, permit greater disclosure, and reach new levels of closeness. Friendships have moments of great intensity. Friends may hurt each other deeply and then feel strong desires to patch up their problems. College friendships may not be easy for an outsider to understand. They are forged in part by a great emotional energy, and the outcomes are not strictly logical.

The quality of friendships and the pattern of developing

friends appear to be different for young men and young women (Bell, 1981; Fischer, 1981). Girls tend to move through three phases in friendship development. In the early phase, from about age eleven to thirteen, friendship is based on *activity*. Young teenage girls look for friends who will do things with them. In the second phase, from about fourteen to sixteen, girls look for friendship based on *loyalty* and *trust*. Friends are people a girl can talk to and confide in—people who will not betray her to others. During this period, girls may have strong feelings of anxiety because they worry about being rejected and abandoned by their friends.

In the third phase, which corresponds to the later high school and college years, *personality* and *shared interests* figure more centrally in young women's friendships. Anxiety about rejection is reduced. College women place greater value on their friends' distinct personality qualities such as warmth or sense of humor. These friendships are characterized by new levels of openness and mutual understanding.

For boys, movement away from activity-based friendships is less marked than it is for girls. College men continue to base close friendships on mutual enjoyment of shared activities. Anxiety about rejection from friends is usually not as intense or prolonged for young men as it is for young women. The level of intimacy and understanding is not as great in friendships between two young men as it is in friendships between two young women, or between a young man and a young woman. For young men, college friendships emphasize companionship and loyalty more than emotional intimacy and self-disclosure.

For some men and women, the friendships made during college have the potential to be deep and lasting. Some adults continue to maintain relationships with friends they made during college. These friends are linked together through the shared experiences of college life, and they continue to share experiences in adulthood. They also share the intimate, common thread of having explored issues of critical personal relevance with one another.

For most people, the friendships formed during college end with graduation. In the process of making friends, however, students form essential views and values about friendship itself. Friendships made during this time provide the foundation for a young adult's approach to lifelong relationships. They are a field for practicing how to make important life commitments.

Remembering Jack Kennedy's friend Lem, we have an example of a person who had a deep commitment to friendship as a life-enriching value.

> In Lem's emotional landscape, friendship was the highest form of devotion. He was committed to friendship as to a covenant, the most important precept of which was ferocious loyalty: You stood by your friend in any circumstance. You defended him against his detractors. You were sympathetic to his opinions. You fought his battles with him. You loved the people he loved, hated those he disliked. You were never away when needed. You covered his weaknesses with your strengths. You accepted his flaws. You did not sit in judgment against him. You suffered no embarrassment from being completely honest. By adhering to such guidelines, you were able to share continuous emotional fidelity and absolute trust. (Michaelis, 1983, p. 185)

FRIENDSHIP AND THE COLLEGE EXPERIENCE

In the transition from high school to college, existing friendship groups are disrupted and new groups take shape. Students have many ways to meet people and make friends in college. The opportunities for friendship and the types of people a student is likely to meet depend on the approach the student takes to college life.

Some students choose to room with former high school friends. They begin college life with greater control over their immediate social contacts, but they do not have as wide a range of peer contacts as they might if they lived in the dormitories.

Some students pledge a fraternity or sorority and join a well-structured friendship system. Students start off by attending a number of rush parties, so they meet the members of a large number of fraternities or sororities. Once they are accepted as a pledge, they are likely to eat, study, and attend social events with other fraternity or sorority members. Usually, the pledge has a big brother or big sister who helps the newcomer cope with the challenges of college life. This person is assigned after meeting the new pledge and is usually someone who likes the new person. In this way, the system promotes friendship between an older and a younger student.

You might think of the Greek system as a structure that ensures its members all the support they need to establish friendships in the new college environment. Through this system, however, college students are likely to restrict their contacts to the young men and women who are already members of this selective network.

Some students live at home and commute to school. They may have opportunities to meet new friends in class or by participating in student-sponsored activities. However, commuter students need to focus more effort on building college friendships than some other students do, since friendships are less likely to develop through chance meetings in the dormitories or during formal fraternity or sorority events.

Most college students experience a period of uncertainty as they meet one another and begin to seek out new friends to replace those they left behind. In some cases, students feel an initial tug of guilt about abandoning their high school friends for new college friends. They may try to hold on to relationships in both worlds through telephone calls, letters, and visits home. A student going to school in his or her hometown may have some difficulty sustaining relationships with the friends who are not going to college. It is important not to underestimate the struggle that is involved in moving from the close peer group of high school to the more individualized friendship groups of college.

Some college students did not develop strong friendships in high school for a number of reasons. Students who were not socially mature may have been left out of the high school crowds. The very bright students, who were more focused on academic success than on popularity, may have found it difficult to feel part of the high school peer group. Some students who move to a new town during the later years of high school have trouble getting into a friendship circle.

For these students, college provides a new opportunity to establish friendships. It brings together people of ability who are more likely to be serious about their academic goals than most high school students are. All of them are experiencing a very similar period of personal and social transition. Exchanging ideas and sharing experiences that occur in college provide a rich context for the formation of friendships. What is more, most college men and women have many excellent social and intellectual skills to contribute to friendship formation. They are better prepared than they were during high school to participate in recip-rocal, respectful, and caring friendships.

Despite the skills that college students bring to friendship formation, the pursuit of friendship still runs into some difficulties. One of the biggest problems students face is the experience of betrayal. Given the new responsibility of keeping the confidence of a close friend, many young people find that they are not up to the trust. Lying to friends and telling a friend's confidences to someone else are common problems that college students encounter. Students may find that people in whom they have placed their trust are not dependable. They may also find that even though they want to be loyal and supportive, they may give in to pressures to deceive or betray their friends.

Behavior in friendship relations is tied to role exploration and the establishment of personal values. Some young adults discover that their commitment to loyalty and openness in a friendship is far more important to them than other values, such as personal achievement or social status. Other young people find that even though they may say they value loyalty in friendship, they are not willing to put their own success or personal recognition aside when it conflicts with a commitment made to a friend. Through the process of forming friendships and dissolving friendships, college students begin to take responsibility for a wide range of moral and ethical actions. Rarely do they find relationships that are as noble and straightforward as they may have hoped.

Sometimes college students become embroiled in self-deception to build friendships. In order to win someone over, a person may try to create a false impression. Over time, the student begins to believe that he or she really has the qualities or values that fit the charade. This process can derail real progress toward identity formation. Students can become so focused on being accepted by some person or group that they deny their true characters.

The process of making friends in college is at least as important, if not more important, than emerging from college with two or three lifelong friends. Through the efforts to build friendships, college students learn a lot about themselves. They begin to put many of their values to the test. In addition, they learn about the characteristics of their peer group. This is the group that will emerge together into the world of adult life. Having gone through some of the negative experiences of betrayal, dishonesty, and self-deception, as well as the positive experiences of loyalty, openness, and support, young people are better prepared to cope with the social realities of impending adulthood.

FRIENDSHIP AND IDENTITY FORMATION

A student at a small New England liberal arts college described the quality of her closest college friendship. This description shows how opening herself up to the vulnerability of intimacy in a friendship helped foster real progress in self-awareness and personal growth.

> "Junior year I formed the closest relationship to anyone I've ever had, not only at Berkshire but anywhere. Lisa and I became extremely close. She cared about what I thought, and many times, even though she had reservations about what I was feeling, she never attacked but asked questions, her questions making me question in turn and generally causing me to at least reevaluate those feelings. We talked hours on end about Berkshire and what was happening to us and everyone else here." (Goethals and Klos, 1986, p. 234)

Several studies suggest the link between friendship formation and personal identity. At first, friendships tend to be based on proximity. Students who live on the same floor or who share a room become friends. After a few months, however, friendships are more likely to be based on common values than on who lives near whom. Students discover other students who are struggling with the same problems and who are committed to similar values.

One of the major value conflicts that college women face is between their occupational goals and their goals for marriage and family life. We know that most married women also work outside the home. However, the decision to set high standards for occupational success and to enter highly competitive fields usually brings with it a decision to delay marriage and perhaps to remain childless. Women who have more traditional values about marriage and family life tend to select occupations that they believe will fit well with these family life values, such as teaching, real estate, and social services.

College women seek friends who can help them resolve this conflict and who will support the position they finally choose. The role of friends is especially critical for women students who are selecting traditionally male-dominated majors or careers such as computer science, engineering, mathematics, or finance. These women need to find male and female friends who encourage their career orientation. Their male friends must support the idea of having a wife who will pursue a career. Their male and female friends must see many benefits and satisfactions in pursuing such a career. Thus, women who have non-traditional career goals need to identify friends who will help them resist the social pressures to follow a more traditional path.

FRIENDSHIPS BETWEEN
YOUNG MEN AND WOMEN

Generally, women's friendships have higher levels of open communication and closeness than do those of men. This is, in part, a result of childhood socialization practices. Our culture places a very high value on interpersonal skill development for girls and women. As young adults, women tend to have more skills for the formation and maintenance of close relationships. Many young men find great satisfaction in their friendships with young women because the communication is more open and there is greater intimacy than in their friendships with men.

You may have trouble understanding how your son or daughter can have a close friendship with a person of the opposite sex. Most of today's adults grew up in an era when opposite-sex friendships were unlikely. Men and women dated, went steady, got engaged, and married; but they were rarely just friends. However, in today's college environment, men and women may live in the same residence halls, be lab partners in science courses, work together in the same clubs and organizations, and collaborate on class projects. Young men and women may share an off-campus apartment, take weekend camping trips together, or drive cross country together, and still be just friends.

Those friendships have many advantages. In today's world of work, men and women are frequently in situations that require collaboration. The college environment provides a setting where men and women can learn to respect each other's competence and work together effectively. Through friendships, young men and women learn to revise their stereotypes about how men and women behave. Women are likely to discover that men can be supportive and understanding. Men are likely to discover that women can be skillful problem solvers. This is clearly an area where our sons and daughters can help us approach relationships from a more flexible perspective.

LONELINESS

College brings new opportunities for friendship, but it also brings new experiences of isolation and loneliness. Many college students leave the comfort and familiarity of their support system at home for a new environment. Others break ties with old friends who have gone to work or entered the military right after high school. The early weeks and months of college are likely to bring deep feelings of isolation and loneliness. These feelings are intensified because students usually approach the transition to college with such positive anticipation. They often do not even consider that this change will bring any sense of uprootedness or loss.

Loneliness is a common experience of college life. An estimated 25 percent of the college population feel extremely lonely at some time during any given month. These feelings are likely to be most noticeable during the freshman year because of the sharp contrast between the structure of high school life and the independence expected of students in college. However, loneliness can be a theme throughout the college years. The process of becoming an individual brings with it a new appreciation for one's separateness from others. As young people discover their own uniqueness, from time to time they are bound to feel that no one else really understands them.

You may find that when your son or daughter is away at college *you* experience periods of loneliness. You miss the physical presence of a person you love. You miss the daily interactions. Your increasing autonomy in the parent-child relationship makes you and your child more separate than you were before. Now and again, you may yearn for things to be more like they were and wish to be less separate.

Loneliness can be classified into three categories: transient, situational, and chronic (Meer, 1985).

Transient loneliness lasts a short time and passes. College students may feel this kind of loneliness when their friends are out on dates and they are alone in the dorm. This type of loneliness may occur when a student is the only one to take a certain position in a discussion; the only black student in a class; or the only one working out in a large, empty gym.

Situational loneliness accompanies a sudden loss or a move to a new city. Students commonly experience this kind of loneliness when they first come to college, especially if they are away from home. Most of us are disoriented when we move to a new town. Going to college is no different. Despite the many new and wonderful facets of college life, most young people experience situational loneliness due to the loss of the supportive, familiar environment of their homes and communities.

As parents, you may undergo situational loneliness because of the loss of your child's presence. Even though you have planned and saved for this opportunity, you may experience intense loneliness following your child's departure. Rather than trying to create a myth that no one is feeling lonely, parents and college students can help each other through this time by admitting their loneliness and doing their best to reduce it. Frequent telephone calls, letters, and visits home in the first few months can ease the feelings of loss.

Chronic loneliness lasts a long time and cannot be linked

to a specific event or situation. Chronically lonely people may have an average number of social contacts, but these contacts are not meaningful in helping the person achieve the desired level of intimacy. Chronically lonely people often seem reluctant to make contact with others. There appears to be a strong relationship between social skills and chronic loneliness. People who have higher levels of social skill, including friendliness, communication skills, appropriate nonverbal behavior, and appropriate response to others, have more adequate social support and experience lower levels of loneliness.

You may not recognize that your child suffers from chronic loneliness until he or she is away at college. While children are living at home, parents are usually able to provide the amount of social support their children need. At college, children may find it extremely difficult to replace the level of trust and closeness that was provided by family members and high school friends.

Inadequate friendship relationships may actually interfere with a student's academic performance as well as his or her physical and mental health. Substantial research evidence supports the relationship between inadequate social support and vulnerability to illness. People who are part of a strong social support system are more likely to resist disease and to recover quickly from illnesses when they occur. Their general outlook on life is more optimistic.

A college student's circle of friends plays a key role in keeping the young person integrated into the social environment. Friends look in on you when you are sick; they make sure you have the assignment if you miss class; they invite you to join them if they are going to a party, a special lecture, or a campus concert. Friends worry about you and remind you to take care of yourself. Friends monitor your moods and prevent you from becoming too preoccupied or too discouraged. Friends value you and support your emerging identity. They understand the importance of the questions you are raising, and they encourage you to say what's on your mind. Building and maintaining satisfying friendships are key ingredients to feeling at home and succeeding in college.

ADDITIONAL READING

Bell, R. R. (1981). *Worlds of friendship.* Beverly Hills, CA: Sage.

McGinnis, A. L. (1979). *The friendship factor.* Minneapolis, MN: Augsburg.

Meer, J. (July, 1985). Loneliness. *Psychology Today,* 19, pp. 28–33.

Michaelis, D. (1983). *The best of friends: Profiles of extraordinary friendships.* New York: William Morrow and Co.

Becoming Men and Women

By the end of high school, most young people have acquired a set of stereotypes about masculinity or femininity. The stereotypes may have been learned from peers, in school, from parents, and through the media. But during college a person begins to question and understand in a more authentic, in-depth way what it really means to be a man or a woman.

Are men strong, tough, aggressive, insensitive, independent, logical, task-oriented, and macho? Are women passive, weak, nurturant, emotional, expressive, dependent, and sensitive to the needs of people in social situations? These are some of the more widely held stereotypes of the masculine and feminine gender roles. College students often come under pressure to behave in accord with the gender-role expectations that are common in our culture. As this is also the time for the discovery of their personal identities, however, individuals now begin to compare themselves with these demands in order to answer the questions, What am I like as a person? How do I compare with the culture's ideal of a man or a woman?

On the one hand, it may be necessary to discard elements of the cultural stereotype because they do not fit one's own makeup. On the other hand, it may be necessary to accept or adapt to some of these stereotypes because they do constitute what other people expect. Gender-role identity is formed as a result of the tension between social expectations and personal tendencies. This takes place through a process of questioning and self-examination. Young people need to reflect on the fit or lack of fit between their own personalities and the messages that come to them about how men and women should behave.

It is difficult to summarize exactly how this process unfolds because there are many different types of people to consider. It is helpful to think of gender identity along two dimensions: biological sex and personal characteristics and preferences.

Biologically, there are males and females. Many people believe that biological sex must make a difference in how a person behaves. Actually, research has identified relatively few areas of consistent and distinct differences in personality, talents, or temperament between males and females. Aside from obvious differences in physical development, including important reproductive differences, many of the differences between men and women appear to be the result of socialization.

With respect to personal characteristics, people can prefer mostly what are considered to be masculine characteristics, mostly what are considered to be feminine characteristics, or a mixture of the two. Preferences for personal characteristics cover a wide range of behaviors. Social norms about gender role include expectations about how men and women should interact with each other, what they should be good at, how they should dress, and how they should express their feelings.

So, some biological males have strong preferences for masculine characteristics, some have strong preferences for some masculine and some feminine characteristics, and some have strong preferences for feminine characteristics. Similarly, some biological females have strong preferences for feminine characteristics, some have strong preferences for some masculine and some feminine characteristics, and some have strong preferences for masculine characteristics.

Our society is varied enough that people with all these patterns are able to build life-styles that can be satisfying. The process of forming gender identity involves coming to accept and value one's feminine and masculine characteristics and to synthesize them into a personal definition of what it means to be a man or a woman.

The process of questioning one's gender role may be somewhat more acceptable for students today than it was forty years ago. Gender characteristics are discussed openly. There is not as much agreement today about what a male should be like or what a female should be like as there was years ago. Put another way, both males and females have more latitude today to consider a wider range of behaviors as appropriate. This leads to greater freedom for self-expression, allowing people to match their own preferences, tendencies, and needs with possible ways of being that are acceptable.

Nevertheless, children and adolescents still confront stereotyped ideas about how men and women ought to behave. Many young men have learned that they should be strong and unemotional, handle their problems on their own, and not allow themselves to be vulnerable to the pain and suffering of relationships. Men are expected to take care of others and not to need to be taken care of.

During the college years, however, your male children will feel weak and vulnerable at times. They will want to be taken care of. They will want others to be sensitive to their feelings. Some young men may be reluctant to admit their feelings because within the male gender-role stereotype those feelings are not acceptable.

As the college years proceed, young men become increasingly aware that these are human needs, not needs associated with being a male or a female. Your male children may begin to understand that they have needs to talk to somebody about deeply personal feelings and to be understood by this other person. They may need to be reassured and comforted, both physically and emotionally. In the process, they may become more accepting of their own needs for expressing their feelings and for accepting the care and concern of others.

Females may feel that they should be sensitive to the needs of others and not be assertive. They may have come under pressure to disguise the full range of their competence, especially to appear attractive to young men. Most college women will discover that they want to assert themselves, to exercise competence, and to assume leadership roles. Although they may feel reluctant to express these feelings and may believe that these needs are inappropriate for women, they will also perceive the benefits and the personal satisfaction that result from expressing themselves in a competent, independent way. This is one of the major conflicts facing female college students today.

According to the results of a national survey conducted by the American Council on Education, of those students entering colleges and universities as freshmen in the fall of 1989, 32 percent of the males thought that a married woman's activities were best confined to the home. About 20 percent of the female students agreed with this statement (Astin, 1989). Even among male and female students who accept the idea that a woman should work outside the home, there is still conflict about just how much investment in a career is appropriate for women. Some women and men consider it unfeminine for women to have far-reaching ambitions. Many students, both male and female, expect that a woman will work after her marriage, but only to provide a secondary income, not to fulfill personally meaningful career goals. The question of how career aspirations are woven into a general life-style is a key problem in the formation of gender identity for college women.

During college, many young women begin to understand that needs for competence and mastery are human needs, needs that are appropriately expressed by both men and women. Women can become comfortable stating their opinions, being self-reliant, and taking the lead in projects or groups. As their expertise in a certain field grows, they can become increasingly confident of their potential as effective professionals.

The way in which young women formulate ideas concerning their investment in career and their investment in marriage and parenthood will be influenced by the examples they have seen in their homes and among their friends. If they fall in love during college, the attitudes and values of their intimate partner will also shape their outlook. However, it has been our observation that female students are not fully able to resolve this issue while they are in college. They simply do not have the full range of experiences in the world of work or in the world of marriage and family life to know how they will react to the demands of these various life roles.

While your children are in college, you are likely to observe them using a variety of methods to explore elements of their own gender-role identity. On occasion, your son may appear to be "macho man" or your daughter may come home as Scarlett O'Hara. You may feel that they have grossly exaggerated the masculine or feminine ideal, or you may feel very pleased with their behavior. At other times, you may sense that they are tentative. You see them as hesitant; truly grappling with the issues of how their own personalities and needs fit with the gender-related expectations of their culture. They are exploring the issues of what is important for men and women in our society. Their exploration will allow them to arrive at a gender-role identity that is comfortable for them within the culture in which they operate.

The exploration of gender-role identity takes place within the context of the college environment. The definitions of acceptable male and female characteristics will vary from one college to another and may differ from how these roles are defined among the adults in your own town or city.

Most campuses are comprised of small subcultures of student groups that create their own norms and standards for behavior. Students who live in a certain sorority or fraternity may come under pressure to dress in a particular style, date only specific types of students, or express shared attitudes and values. Other pressures may be imposed by students in a dormitory, in a student club, or on an athletic team.

Sometimes your son or daughter may fit in just fine with these expectations and restrictions. Other times they may chafe against these expectations as they attempt to assert their own individuality and enter a period of exploration. Over the course of four or five years of college, students may question the groups they are in and shift from one social group to another as they examine and construct their own gender-role identities. These tensions are not bad in and of themselves. They are part of a process through which college students come to understand themselves and their culture and through which they formulate a way to comfortably accommodate the two.

College life involves a great variety of experiences that can contribute to the clarification of gender-role identity. As an example, students may be required to spend time with infants, toddlers, and young children in a day-care center or preschool as part of a course in psychology, education, or child development. Through this experience, students have the opportunity to develop their skills in nurturing, observing, and effectively communicating with young children.

The experience can help both males and females understand the complex demands of parenting and can help them identify their potential talents as teachers and caregivers. Placed in an arena where the ability to be sensitive to the needs of others as well as to exercise leadership and responsibility are encouraged, both male and female students can examine some of their own talents and feelings in the face of some of the common stereotypes about gender.

Male and female students will need to confront gender stereotypes in many situations to succeed in college. Some courses require high levels of competition; some courses require group cooperation and high levels of teamwork; some teachers expect students to be assertive, and they give attention only to those students who speak out. Students may find themselves in leadership positions in student organizations, in their residence halls, or in their fraternities or sororities, where they must combine the skills of being sensitive to the needs of others with skills for asserting their views and taking some responsibility for the guidance of others. Students who want to be effective have to learn to use those interpersonal skills and personal resources that are most appropriate to the situation. Their gender-role definitions have to be flexible enough to permit them to develop a broad array of social strategies. Over time, students may decide that there are no reasons to restrict their social interactions because of their gender.

If we look back to the 1950s, the life scripts for men and women were more clearly laid out, especially in the middle class. Husbands were expected to be the breadwinners; wives were expected to be homemakers and mothers. Competence was expected to be exercised by men and women in their different domains. Women were concerned about furthering their husbands' careers, often making vital contributions to their success. Men and women married relatively young, had children soon after marriage, and expected their marriages to remain intact. Only a small percentage of adults in the 1950s had a college education. Very few adults elected voluntary childlessness as a life-style option, and very few adults chose to remain single.

What has emerged today and what faces us in the 1990s is a world of many more options. There are life scripts for a variety of adult life-styles that can be both personally satisfying and socially valued.

Some people elect a life-style similar to the one that was predominant in the 1950s, with a traditional division of responsibilities for the man and the woman. However, this is a far smaller number of people, and this script no longer describes the majority of adult households.

In the majority of families, even families with small children, both husbands and wives are employed outside the home. This life-style, sometimes referred to as the dual-earner couple, provides more financial resources. This life-style also has more strain involved, as couples try to balance more demands in the same amount of time.

Today, many young people begin to pursue careers after they graduate from college and delay getting married until their late twenties or longer. This means that both men and women seem to be involved in establishing their careers and exploring their talents. When they do marry, both partners are likely to have an investment in their separate careers. They may postpone having children until they are in their thirties or forties, allowing themselves some time to be together as a married couple. The babies born to these older couples often turn out to be healthier than babies born to very young mothers. They appear to benefit from the educational advantage of their parents and are vulnerable to fewer risks than children born to young parents.

After having children, many women decide to remain at home and return to their careers when their children are a bit older. Other women return to work shortly after a child is born. With the support of their husbands and the use of child-care professionals, they strive to balance the demands of work and family life. Some women modify their work roles by doing more work at home or working part-time while their children are young. Companies are beginning to adapt to this variety of solutions by permitting greater flexibility for mothers who want to combine work and parenting. More men are also assuming greater responsibility for child care.

Of course, some people get married while they are in college or right after college. These couples forge their careers, their families, and the balance between work and family within the context of their marriages. A large group of young adults remains single by choice. Some of them choose to raise children. Some people elect to establish a life-style with a same-sex partner. Others elect to live with a heterosexual partner but not to marry. The high divorce rate results in a large number of single-parent families.

This variety of life-styles is a reflection of a changing

society in which a greater range of individual needs is permitted to be expressed and fulfilled. Gender roles are being reworked to accommodate greater individual differences. This allows society to take advantage of the full range of talents of women as well as men. It also places fewer individuals in categories that stigmatize them with negative labels that might reduce their full participation in their communities.

In the postcollege years, prior to marriage or the choice of a life partner, the most important single factor in the successful development of any of the varied life-styles is a supportive social network that validates a person's choices and efforts. Friends, coworkers, and neighbors play a key role by suggesting that a person's decisions—to pursue a career, to marry or remain single, to have children or to remain childless, to place priority on career ambitions or on family life, to establish a gay or lesbian relationship—are sensible for the individual. Knowing that people are striving to understand an individual and to help this person establish a meaningful life-style is fundamental to providing the sense of security necessary to accomplish the task.

Once a person makes a decision about an intimate life partner, that partner often becomes the single most powerful voice in providing support or opposition to critical life decisions. All the efforts that have gone into exploring gender-role identity come to bear in helping a person form, sustain, and continue to enhance a loving, intimate, supportive relationship in adulthood. The understanding and commitment of each partner to the family, career, and personal needs of the other, and the willingness of each partner to help foster continued growth in each of these areas for one another, are what make it possible for a couple to build a fulfilling life together.

COLLEGE ROMANCE

A powerful form of gender-role exploration occurs during the college years as young people experience loving relationships. Love is one of the more intense human emotions. It is not fleeting but persists over hours, days, and years. For people who are falling in love, the emotion can be quite distracting, taking their thoughts away from other tasks and forcing them to alter the course of their behavior. A college student may sit down to study and find himself drawn into powerful fantasies about the person he loves. A student may find herself consumed with jealousy watching the person she loves interact with someone else. Students may experience anxiety about the safety of those they love if they are late in calling or showing up for a date. A student may feel intense joy in the presence of the person he or she loves.

The intensity and fullness of emotions associated with love brings young people into contact with a whole range of feelings that may be new and surprising. Students who have not had experiences with a close, loving relationship in high school may feel more confused, even overwhelmed, by these emotions than students who have had these experiences. Even for someone who has had high school romances, a new, intense romance may become an overwhelming preoccupation. Young men in particular, who have been socialized to limit the expression of their emotions, may find it difficult to understand or express how they feel.

Falling in love always brings with it the potential for a new set of personal understandings about the depth and variety of an individual's emotional life. As much as falling in love is about caring for someone else, during college it is also about becoming acquainted with an important element of a student's own identity.

College romances may present an early challenge when they disrupt love relationships that were established in high school. Many students are still involved with a serious boyfriend or girlfriend from high school when they begin college. They may think that this high school relationship will continue. They telephone, write, and spend time with one another on special weekends home and during vacation. Sometimes the partners have chosen to attend the same college, so they see each other daily.

You may know some couples who fell in love in high school and then married during or after college. Actually, this is very unusual. Once students become involved in the new, complex, and diverse environment of college life, they find new friends and create a new vision of themselves and their futures. Their feelings for their high school partners are likely to change as they change.

Drifting apart can be confusing, even painful, especially if it occurs for one partner and not the other. During the freshman year, young people are tempted to hold onto their high school romances as a source of stability amidst a great deal of change. They may use these relationships as a safe harbor while they take risks in exploring many other aspects of college life. They can avoid the risks of possible social rejection by telling themselves and others that they are being faithful to their high school partner by not trying to meet new people.

Students may confuse feelings of familiarity and safety with love. Then, as a new romance develops, they may feel guilty about abandoning the earlier relationship. They may question the sincerity of their earlier feelings. How could they have felt so committed to someone just a few months ago, and now be so eager for a new relationship?

Even if a new romance does not develop, college students begin to take a new view of how they want to be treated by a person of the opposite sex and what they want out of a loving relationship. Young men and women may become impatient with the extreme dependence of their high school partners. They may feel that their partners are inconsiderate of their feelings or are not really ready to be open about important thoughts and feelings. They may feel that they are being treated as sex objects and not really valued for other important abilities. They may discover that their partners lack integrity and are not willing to be honest with them.

Sometimes these high school relationships become rather destructive. For whatever reason, one partner may begin to try to control, exploit, or dominate the other. This can be torturous. A student at college may become so distracted by the turn of events that he or she is unable to concentrate on school work or to build a social life among a new group of peers. He or she may be too wrapped up in the relationship to see the problems in it. At that point, parents must try to step in to help the young person take a more objective view of the relationship and the direction things are going. Parents can help students stay on course academically and advise them to gain some distance. Friends can also be helpful in this regard.

As young people become critical of their early love relationships, they learn essential lessons about their gender-role identity. They explore the limits of what they are willing to give and what they are willing accept in order to sustain a love relationship.

As parents, you can appreciate that the dissolution of high school romances is a normal part of growing up. You understand how unlikely it is for those relationships to endure. You may even see that holding on to those relationships and spending too much time on them may prevent a young person from taking full advantage of the opportunities and experiences of college.

From this perspective, you can reassure your child that it is natural to move on to new relationships. It is not a sign of immaturity or an inability to establish enduring love relationships. In fact, the ability to fall in love and care for someone shows the budding of a basic human capacity for tenderness that can be expected to grow in depth and compassion over the years, although not necessarily with the same partner.

During the college years, most young men and women hope to find a close, loving relationship. Even if falling in love is not mentioned in the course bulletin or in the college recruitment materials, it is part of what most students expect to happen at college. For college students, the search for a loving relationship is a search to satisfy needs for understanding, emotional closeness, and physical intimacy. As they become clearer about their own personal identity, students want to know that they are capable of giving and receiving love. They are asking whether the newly formulated vision of themselves that is taking shape can be valued and cherished by anyone else.

Within the context of a loving relationship, college students experience growth in self-understanding at the same time that they become more capable of meeting the needs of someone else. Students may find themselves attracted to partners from very different home and family backgrounds from their own. Students may discover that they care about those who have very different religious or political views from their own. They may find that the people they care about have very different definitions of personal success and happiness from their own. Although most people eventually marry someone who is relatively similar to themselves in these respects, these relationships provide opportunities to examine closely some other ways of seeing the world.

> Andrea was interested in the varieties of her new friends' ways of thinking; she seemed to be in search of a vehicle by which to achieve independence from her parents. It came in the form of a man with whom she developed a serious relationship in her sophomore year. Arnold seemed to be a lot like her but more self-assured. He was supportive of her ambitions and desire for education and consoled and encouraged her when she felt pressured or worried about her future. "He made me more sure of myself, more self-confident and willing to try new things. It was important just having someone there who thought a lot of me. He helped me to grow up." (Josselson, 1987, p. 84)

One of the very challenging discoveries that can take place during college is that one prefers sexual partners of the same sex. About 5 to 10 percent of men are gay, and about 5 percent of women are lesbians. In addition, there are men and women who are bisexual or who have experimented with homosexual relationships. Even though homosexuality is discussed more openly than in the past, college students who are openly gay or lesbian are often targets of hostility, rejection, and ridicule. The commitment to a gay or lesbian sexual orientation is usually reached only after a period of intense introspection. Many students try to deny this conclusion and withdraw from social relationships. Others find support in their decision from students, faculty, or staff who have resolved their conflicts about their sexual orientation and find positive ways of forming intimate relationships with same-sex partners.

Young people find new opportunities to examine many of the assumptions they have had about their personal identities as part of becoming close to someone. Because they care about this other person, they are more willing to open up to the new ideas this person might suggest. They are more willing to rethink their own beliefs. As the partners reach each new level of closeness, they have to assess their continued compatibility. The more they learn about one another, the more they learn about themselves.

One of the invigorating aspects of finding someone you love who loves you in return is that you can be so entirely yourself. College students are likely to begin their social life by trying to create an image or an impression that they think will work. As one facet of role experimentation, they try out different styles and airs that they hope will be attractive. They may even develop a relationship with someone who is drawn in by this facade. But over time, this game playing wears thin.

As young people become more confident about who they are and what they hope to become, they want to be free to present themselves in the most authentic way possible. They want to mean the same thing to someone else as they are coming to mean to themselves. When they find someone else who seems not only to accept but to cherish this newly formed vision of the self, a deep well of loving feelings can be released.

The expectations students have about romantic relationships depend, in part, on preexisting values. The more young men and women base their gender roles on traditional values about separate and distinct roles that men and women are expected to play in work and family life, the more they are likely to value infatuation in a romantic relationship. They are looking for a man or woman who will complete their personalities. Falling in love creates a whole system by bringing together two incomplete but complementary sets of qualities.

In contrast, young men and women who have more egalitarian values about gender roles tend to emphasize trust and mutual understanding as the basis for love. They are looking for a love relationship that offers support and compassion as well as physical closeness. They are less likely to trust infatuation and more likely to expect high levels of openness and frankness in an intimate partner.

It is difficult to predict whether a love relationship established in college will lead to marriage. Most students do not expect to get married while they are in college. Those students who have plans for postgraduate study generally do not expect to get married right after college. So a love relationship might be very intense, and the couple may feel very deeply about one another yet not intend to marry.

It makes sense to view these romances as explorations in the capacity for commitment, both commitment to gender identity and commitment to an intimate relationship. The college years are a time when young people are developing a new sense of autonomy. They make many decisions on their own, exercise independent judgment, and assert their own ideas and opinions. As part of falling in love and sustaining a loving relationship, young men and women have to explore the many dimensions of closeness. They discover how much they are willing to reveal about themselves to the other person. They discover what they are willing to sacrifice or postpone in order to help and support the other person. They discover what gives them pleasure and how to give pleasure to someone else. They explore the dynamics of mutuality as they try to regulate their own needs and desires with the needs and desires of the other person so that both partners can be satisfied. Forging a new sense of independence and forging a new level of mutuality may not be exactly compatible. The level of closeness a couple can achieve during the college years depends on how much each partner has already satisfied his or her needs for independence and how much of this independence each is willing to modify for the satisfactions of intimacy.

Young men and women face many of the same challenges, and some that are distinct, in building a loving relationship. Men and women have to answer many of the following questions in order to find out what it means to make a commitment to a relationship. What do they have to give up to keep the relationship going, and are they willing to do that? How do they expect to be treated by their intimate partners? Do they take pride and pleasure in the successes and accomplishments of their partners, and do the partners take pride and pleasure in their successes? Are they willing to stand by their partners when things are not going very well, to be supportive at times when their partners cannot give much in return? Will the partners do this for them?

Beyond these common issues, the greatest challenges in building a love relationship for young men are related to expressiveness and disclosure. Typically, young men are not as accustomed as young women to talking about personal matters, exploring their feelings, and listening to the personal concerns of others. A young man may feel that he is really opening up and reaching a new level of personal closeness with his girlfriend, yet she may feel that their conversations are still superficial. She may want to know more about his private thoughts and feelings than he is willing or even able to provide. She may expect him to want to know her private thoughts and feelings. He may feel that pressures for greater levels of self-disclosure threaten his sense of independence and create uncomfortable feelings of vulnerability.

The greatest challenges in building a love relationship for young women are related to preserving a sense of personal identity. Many young women are especially sensitive to trying to meet the needs of their partners. They want to say and do those things that will create a feeling of harmony for the couple. A young woman may say things she does not really mean or do things she does not really enjoy in order to please her boyfriend. She may feel that if she asserts herself, she will be rejected. She may be tempted to place her personal identity in a position subordinate to that of her boyfriend. Her boyfriend may think that everything is going well and that she is very happy, but she may find herself feeling increasingly isolated in the relationship.

As parents, you must play your role in relation to your child's love relationships very cautiously. Most college-age children hope for parental approval of their romantic partners, but they probably will not ask openly for this approval. Too much parental enthusiasm about a relationship may be perceived by the couple as pressure to marry. The couple may respond by backing away from the relationship. Too much parental criticism can stimulate a greater commitment to the relationship than might otherwise be there. The couple may cling together more urgently because of their perception that their parents are trying to break them up. You do not want to push your child into a marriage that is motivated primarily by a desire to rebel against your parental control. Thus, your best move here is to be courteously neutral in your response to your child's romantic partner, not expressing much preference one way or the other.

As parents, you have another role to play when the romantic relationship comes to an end. The intensity of loving feelings brings with it the possibility of a deep sense of personal loss when the relationship ends. Parents usually want to protect their children from pain. You can anticipate, however, that if your child is capable of experiencing the mature feelings of love, he or she will become vulnerable to feelings of grief when an intimate companion is lost.

As a caring parent, you must be available to offer comfort. Even if you believe that the relationship needed to end, even if you feel that the match was not a good one, you must be aware that your child is likely to be experiencing profound and troubling emotions when a love has ended. You can help by taking the time to listen, by acknowledging your child's feelings, and by reserving your own views about the situation until your child can understand how he or she feels. You can offer reassurance and optimism about future relationships. You can help your child appreciate the importance of the capacity for love in the broad scope of personal development. Each opportunity to experience a loving, caring relationship is a chance to participate in the best of human nature, a chance to take one step closer to the human ideal.

ADDITIONAL READING

Doyle, J. A. and Paludi, M. A. (1991). *Sex and gender: The human experience*. Dubuque, IA: Wm. C. Brown.

Griffin, C. W., Wirth, M. J., and Wirth, A. G. (1986). *Beyond acceptance: Parents of lesbians and gays talk about their experiences*. Englewood Cliffs, NJ: Prentice-Hall.

Josselson, R. (1987). *Finding herself: Pathways to identity development in women*. San Francisco: Jossey-Bass.

Kimmel, M. S. (Ed.) (1987). *Changing men: New directions in research on men and masculinity.* Newbury Park, CA: Sage.

McGinnis, A. L. (1982). *The romance factor.* San Francisco: Harper and Row.

Perlman, D. and Duck, S. (1987). *Intimate relationships: Development, dynamics, and deterioration.* Newbury Park, CA: Sage.

Career
Selection and
Commitment

The occupational demands of our society create a persistent pressure for self-examination. Students need to have opportunities to analyze their abilities and interests. They need to take pride in their strengths and decide whether they are going to try to improve their weaknesses or simply learn to live with them.

As a result of progress made in forming a personal identity, college students become more confident about their personal attributes and goals. Once they have accepted their emotional and interpersonal needs and strengths, young people are freer to make commitments to a vision of themselves as workers who can achieve future career goals and make significant contributions to their communities. Experimentation with commitments to work may begin in college or even earlier. In contemporary American culture, however, long-lasting commitments to an occupational identity do not become fully formed until later in adulthood.

LIFELONG OCCUPATIONAL CAREER

A lifelong occupational career is a continuously changing set of activities. It is a product of changing competences, emerging goals, and a revised appreciation for the meaning of certain types of work and their related rewards. From this point of view, it does not make sense to expect that a career decision made when someone is age eighteen to twenty-two will endure throughout adulthood without modification. Even if this decision is made in a rational, planned way, using a broad range of information about personal abilities and the characteristics of specific work roles, it is not likely to be a permanent career choice.

As adults grow and change, their awareness of possibilities and their appreciation of their own skills also change. What is more, the labor market is continuously changing. Some jobs are phased out, and new ones emerge. Students must learn to view their college career decisions from a life-span perspective. They must come to understand that what they are choosing is a beginning, an initial position from which to enter the world of work. They must use their college education to learn how to make use of resources, evaluate information, and ask good questions so they can revise their decisions as they move through life. Initially, college students find it difficult to accept such a perspective. They are eager to prove themselves and to establish their credibility in the world of work.

As parents, you have a longer-range perspective on life than your child does. You can be of great help in encouraging your children to take the long-range view of their careers. Students tend to be anxious about careers when they start college. They worry about whether they will make a good choice of a major, whether they will do well in their course work, and whether they will be able to find jobs when they graduate.

As adults who have been involved in the work force for some time, you can provide insight into this aspect of the future that appears so troubling. You know that a college education is going to serve students in many ways, not just to help them get jobs. Their years at college are important for developing a sense of personal identity, a mature gender role, friendships, an informed outlook on politics, science, and technology, a sense of appreciation and satisfaction in the artistic and expressive aspects of our culture, and a vision of a better life for themselves, their families, and future generations. Knowing all this, you can encourage your child's full exploration and use of the college environment and help your child remain focused on the broadest possible view of the value of a college education.

CHOOSING A MAJOR

To graduate from a college or university, a student must complete some general education requirements and the course work in a major area of study. This is true at just about every college or university. Majors are designed by the faculty in the academic departments. Departments are the subject matter areas into which the entire college curriculum is divided. The subject matter areas at your student's college are presented in the college catalog along with the basic requirements for graduation and majors.

Majors are developed to reflect current thinking about the foundations of the field. A major includes a sequence of courses that has been designed to give a student the depth of knowledge and experience necessary to understand the basic content of an area of knowledge, to become familiar with methods of research, scholarship, and/or creative inquiry used in the field, and to become acquainted with the current controversies and emerging issues of the field. In many fields, the course of study in a major will include some direct experience in the application of knowledge, such as an internship, a research apprenticeship, a supervised field placement, or laboratory experimentation.

Majors are not the same as careers. Majors may lead to careers. In some fields, like teaching, nursing, and engineering, there is a very close link between the course work a student takes and the profession the student hopes to enter upon graduation. In some of these professional fields, when students graduate they have a degree and they qualify for a certificate or license that permits them to practice their profession. However, not all students who receive a professional license or certificate upon graduation choose to enter that field. Not all students who major in education become teachers and not all students who major in engineering become engineers.

In most fields, the decision to major in a subject leaves the choice of a career fairly open. For example, a student might decide to major in philosophy. This is excellent preparation for many careers that require logical analysis of problems, the ability to evaluate arguments critically, and the ability to reason about basic issues of ethics and values. Students who major in philosophy may decide to go on in law, business, human relations, or international affairs, to name a few possibilities. They may decide to continue their education in philosophy by going to graduate school and studying for their doctorate in philosophy. But majoring in philosophy is not the same thing as deciding to become a philosopher.

Most students are uncertain about their majors

Some students come to college thinking they already know what they want to major in and what career they will pursue. This feels very comfortable. In comparison to the students who have not yet decided on a major, these students appear confident and in control of their destiny. Other students come to college without a clear idea of the direction they will pursue. They expect to encounter new opportunities and to discover new talents and abilities while they are at college.

Both types of students are likely to experience some changes. At Ohio State University, between 55 percent and 70 percent of each freshman class changes its major during the first year. Most students change their majors at least three times while they are at college. Parents and students should learn to expect this amount of change and redefinition of goals. It is both understandable and necessary as part of the larger process of identity exploration.

Large research universities may offer majors in as many as one hundred academic departments or more. Some departments offer three or four different subspecialities within the same general subject matter area. For example, within the Department of Sociology at Ohio State, some students are studying criminal justice, some are studying demography, and some are studying family sociology. This amount of choice may not be available at every college. But in almost all cases, students will encounter a much broader range of possible areas of specialization in college than in high school.

What is more, students will see men and women as role models working in a variety of fields. They will probably see men teaching courses and conducting research in fields that they may have considered to be traditionally female, such as home economics, art, and dance. They will probably see women teaching courses and conducting research in fields that they may have considered to be traditionally male areas, such as engineering, finance, and physics. Faculty role models demonstrate new possibilities for students as well as confirming previously formed ideas. As a result, students who have considered some subjects inappropriate or unattainable because of their gender, may realize that it is possible to pursue their interests.

As students explore the resources of the college environment, they have an opportunity to awaken new interests as well as to test the strength of earlier preferences. Most colleges and universities have a required core of general education courses that students take during their first two years. During this period of exposure to new ideas and disciplines, students are likely to discover new talents and interests.

Students who start out being very certain about their majors and their eventual careers are likely to undergo questioning and uncertainty during college. This happens as they learn more about the realities of the field they have chosen, as they discover more about their talents and interests, and as they are presented with new fields they knew nothing about. Their uncertainty may be uncomfortable, but it is valuable.

Take the example of a student who came to college thinking she would major in computer science and go into the computer field. This goal emerged during a computer course in high school. The student's parents, teachers, and high school counselor all supported her ambition. The prevailing job market offers excellent career opportunities in this field. However, during her second year at college she took a course in industrial design. Initially, she took the course only to fulfill a requirement. But the teacher was impressive, and the student experienced a distinct sense of satisfaction in completing the assignments for the course. On the teacher's recommendation, the young woman enrolled in the next, more advanced course in industrial design to explore the field further.

The student began a process of self-assessment as well as an assessment of the career paths that lay ahead. Suddenly a matter that she thought was resolved, a decision that was made, had come unraveled. This became an opportunity for the student to evaluate her own personal values, abilities, and goals in the context of the decision about a major. She had to take hold of her own destiny. This is a key element in the process of identity formation as well as in building a sense of how to attain a satisfying occupational career. The decision, in all probability, strengthened her character. In addition, she may encounter similar decisions in the future. Faced with these choices, she will be more capable of making a decision that supports her identity.

Students who start college still undecided about their majors or their career goals also go through a difficult period of decision making. These students have not rejected many of the alternatives that are open to them. Many possible paths lie ahead. Yet there is not time to sample all the majors and subspecialities at the university.

For these students, the first year or two of college requires an active process of gathering and evaluating information. Many colleges offer a freshman-level course in career planning or include information on career exploration in a freshman seminar. In addition to gaining information in the courses in which they are enrolled, students gather information from friends, people they meet, advisors, and family. They may do some self-guided career exploration through computer programs or self-paced re-sources available at the library. They may take interest or ability tests at the college's career counseling center. Stu-dents use feedback about their interests and abilities to help them make decisions. They use the feedback from instructors to determine whether they have the talent to pursue certain fields. Individual instructors who take a special interest in their students can do much to influence their decisions.

Most students who approach college this way are truly enriched by the opportunities for wide-ranging explora-tion. Once they decide on majors, they retain a healthy appreciation for the variety of disciplines they have sampled. They also feel they have satisfied their curiosity about a number of fields before bringing their decision about a major to a close.

Whether students begin with their choice of major and move to another choice, or consider a variety of majors, they are engaging in an active process of information pro-cessing and decision making. They compare emerging ideas about themselves against the content of an academic knowledge base and its related careers. This is an impor-tant psychological process that, at its best, will establish a good fit and the ability to make good choices in work life.

Some students have trouble deciding

The hardest part of this process is closing off some options in favor of others. Some students find this espe-cially difficult. As they are drawn to one area, they begin to worry about abandoning another. They realize that choosing one path means that they will probably have to give up their future in another. No single path is so compel-ling that they can pursue it wholeheartedly. Sometimes this produces a pattern of frequent switching from one major to another. They make little progress toward developing the confidence and expertise that accompany academic success.

Students cannot graduate from college without declaring and completing a major. No matter how many credits they accumulate, they must finally focus on a program of study that will impose some requirements unique to its field. Students in each major are required to enroll in sequences of courses that vary from one discipline to the next. It is not possible to change majors too many times without lengthening the time necessary to complete a degree. Students who experience chronic indecision may continue to perform adequately in their courses, yet they may not be making progress toward a degree because they are shifting from one field to another.

As parents, it is important to assess whether your child is experiencing a healthy period of intellectual exploration or a more serious inability to come to terms with the responsibility of making a significant decision. If you think your child is stuck in a cycle of anxious indecision, you may need to intervene. You probably should take the opportunity to talk with your child at some length about the decision-making process involved in selecting a major. Listen carefully and try to understand why he or she is having difficulty selecting one field over others. As you begin to understand your child's dilemma, you can determine whether the problem lies with the college, the student, or some combination of the two.

Sometimes the student's difficulties are related to a structural feature of the college or major in which the student is trying to enroll. For example, some departments will not accept a student into their program until the student has completed certain prerequisite courses at high levels of performance. If a student misses the chance to enroll in a prerequisite course, or if the student does not perform well in that course, entry into the major may be delayed or even denied. If this is the case, you might suggest a conference with the student's advisor, the department chair, or the person who is responsible for undergraduate admissions in that field. You want the student to understand as clearly as possible what must be done to meet departmental admissions requirements and what alternatives are possible if these requirements cannot be met.

You may discover that the problem involves the student's lack of confidence about being able to succeed in a particular field. In that case, you might suggest a conference with an academic advisor or career counselor. A staff member who has been trained in career development can assess your child's abilities and interests in order to determine whether objective support exists for the direction he or she has chosen. The counselor can also help your child identify related areas of interest or help your child develop greater assertiveness so that the student can approach the decision about a major with more confidence.

Finally, through conversations with your child, you may decide that he or she is not yet ready to make the kind of commitment to academic work that a college program requires. Young people differ in their readiness to make commitments. Some students are just not able to come to closure on these decisions within the time frame that a college program requires. Some students decide to leave college for a while in order to clarify their goals. After discovering more about the world of work and its demands, many students return to college with a new appreciation for a college education and a greater commitment to pursuing a degree. Although leaving college may seem like a drastic choice, sometimes it is the best one to help the student gain the focus, experience, and confidence necessary to make these complicated decisions.

CHOOSING A CAREER

Choosing a major and choosing a career are related, but not identical, decisions. It might be helpful to think of choosing a major as practice for choosing a career. Choosing a major is a much more limited decision, one that has fewer long-range consequences than choosing a career. Most careers are accessible through a variety of educational paths. Students who are interested in studying law after they graduate from college can major in one of many disciplines and be well prepared to apply to law school. Similarly, students who want to work in a social service agency can approach this career from a large number of college majors.

When students choose a major, they are making a commitment for only two or three years of study. They do not have to worry about such things as salary, work conditions, opportunities for career advancement, retirement benefits, and so on. They do not have to think much about demands of their major on their social or family lives. They do not have to worry about whether they will be expected to travel, whether there will be rapid technological advances, or whether the major will retain its status value over the coming ten to twenty years.

Decisions about a major are usually made by the end of the second year of college. Career exploration may begin quite early, even in the preschool years, when children fantasize about possible careers they will pursue when they grow up. But for students who go to college, clarification of the implications of certain career choices generally does not begin in earnest until the student is involved in a major. Sometime toward the end of the junior year and in the senior year, some significant career decisions are made.

A career can be thought of as any composite of work experiences that permits a person to use talents and skills productively. The career of an artist, for example, could involve work in many media, including oil painting, sculpture, ceramics, sketching, collage, watercolor, and pen and ink. The artist may spend some time teaching, some time arranging for exhibits, and some time in creative production of artwork. It is not the medium, the project, or the theme of the work that defines the career, but the artist's personal use of all these activities as the expression of a distinct set of talents and goals.

As long as a person continues to pursue some kind of work, he or she continues to have an occupational career in the broadest sense. Changes in work activities are extremely likely. In contemporary society, workers typically make five to seven occupational shifts in a lifetime. Careers are not defined as much by the workplace, organization, or profession as they are by the individual's perception of meaningful links among various kinds of work he or she has performed. These work-related activities help the person strengthen valued abilities and achieve significant life goals. Personal identity provides a framework for imposing meaning on all these work-related activities.

Factors that influence career decisions

College students believe that their own individual interests, abilities, attitudes, and expectations are the most important factors to consider when thinking about their careers. To be sure, the most common approach to career selection is to try to match the demands and requirements of a certain type of work with an individual's own talents, interests, and skills. As a result of experiences both in the classroom and in other aspects of college life, students become confident about their own talents and interests. They can evaluate their abilities in relation to those of their peers, and in relation to standards that are set by their professors. They also begin to understand which types of tasks and activities bring forth their greatest energy and which types of tasks are tedious or even anxiety producing for them.

By reading these signals, students develop judgment about their capacity to succeed in certain areas as well as their desire or motivation to succeed. Students are likely to believe that their sense of competence as well as their interest and motivation are the only things that are important to consider in making a career decision.

At least five other factors, in addition to individual abilities, interests, and motivation, influence career decision making (O'Neil, Ohlde, Tollefson, et al., 1980). They are family, chance situations, society, social class, and personality. You can help your children take a more realistic look at the full range of factors that influence their decisions. In some cases, the factors deserve more attention than your child may be giving them. In other cases, some factors may be playing too great a part, and you may want to urge your child to minimize or reduce their contribution to decisions.

Family factors. Career decisions are influenced by family factors. Students draw from childhood experiences as they decide their career direction. They may recall projects and activities that were especially satisfying. They may have developed skills or special hobbies that become the basis for a career. In some families, children get their first insights into the world of work by helping their parents with the work they do.

Your children have been making observations about you, their parents, as workers. The satisfaction or lack of satisfaction you have expressed about your work; the kinds of accomplishments you have made; and the way your work is valued by other family members, the community, and the student's peer group, all provide pieces of information that young people carry with them from their families as they face their own career choices.

Some young people are more influenced by their families' values and aspirations than others. In some cases, children appear to come to college primarily to fulfill their parents' dreams. For example, a student may say that he can consider only a major in business. His parents have sent him to college to become an accountant. Any other alternative is unacceptable. If the student cannot be admitted to the accounting major, if the student does poorly in accounting course work, or if the student does not like accounting, the student may feel that the whole purpose of coming to college is lost. It is your job to help your children understand your expectations for them as clearly as possible and to release them from unrealistic demands when necessary.

Students are influenced by the involvement of their parents in the world of work. In particular, students whose mothers are employed outside the home tend to have fewer stereotyped views of careers. Both male and female children whose mothers are employed are more supportive of the idea that women should actively pursue careers. Female students whose mothers have been employed outside the home are also more willing to consider nontraditional career alternatives for themselves.

Values about family life also influence career decisions. In particular, women who have strong traditional family values, including wanting to marry and have children, are likely to consider careers that permit flexible schedules. Women who do not place a central value on marriage and child rearing for themselves are likely to explore a wider range of career options, especially careers that are traditionally male dominated.

Situational Factors. Although students may minimize the role that chance plays in their career decisions, you know that this factor may enter the picture in some way or other. Many uncontrollable events can occur during college that can have a bearing on career direction.

A student may find a job in an on-campus office that suggests a new career direction. A roommate may introduce a student to a career possibility because of his or her family's background and interests. A teacher or academic advisor may take a special interest in a student and identify an internship, a fellowship, or encourage a student to consider graduate school in order to continue in a specific field. In all these examples, new doors are opened as chance exposes the students to options not previously considered.

Chance can play a part in having doors close as well. As a result of a poorly taught course or an intolerant professor, a student may decide not to pursue a field of study. Students may get closed out of courses that are required for a certain program and decide to go in another direction rather than delay their graduation. Students may receive negative feedback from one faculty member and, as a result of that opinion, may conclude that they do not have the talent to pursue a certain career.

As you consider the role that chance can play in career decisions, you may want to advise your child to evaluate these factors carefully. If chance opens doors, it makes sense to take advantage of the opportunities. However, if chance closes doors, students should be cautioned against retreating from important goals.

Societal factors. Each student attends college during a specific historical era. The societal factors that come into play in shaping career decisions change from one era to the next. Consider the following example: In the United States, more than 225,000 students graduate each year with a bachelor's degree in business. More than 65,000 students receive a master's degree in business each year (U.S. Bureau of the Census, 1985). This means that students who aspire to a business career today are likely to face much stronger expectations for a college degree and a major in some aspect of business, management, or administrative science than was the case twenty years ago. In the past, it was much easier to pursue a career in business after having simply graduated from college. Now students have to demonstrate a commitment to a business career by selecting a major in a related field.

In addition, many employment markets are cyclical. For example, right now we have a critical shortage of mathematicians and scientists. You may recall that after the Russian success in launching Sputnik in the 1950s, the United States set about to interest youth in careers in science and engineering. The impact of that effort was a swelling of enrollments in engineering and science programs in the late 1960s and a brief glut in the engineering market in the 1970s. As a result of the glut, funding to support training in the sciences was cut back. Today, many of the graduate students in doctoral programs in engineering, mathematics, and the physical sciences are from foreign countries. American students are not particularly interested in careers in mathematics and physical science, especially careers that require doctoral-level training. The current job market for scientists and engineers is expanding, so career opportunities in those fields are now excellent.

As students consider career alternatives, it does not hurt to understand the career marketplace. This is not to say that a person should avoid areas where the supply is greater than the demand. Every field always has room for the best; and there are never enough of the best to go around. In addition, the relationship between the number of people pursuing a career and the number of available positions fluctuates. However, students should try to anticipate the level of competition they are going to face in finding suitable employment when they graduate. What is more, students may need to consider some career alternatives just in case it proves difficult to enter a specific field immediately upon graduation.

Another consideration is the unevenness of the marketplace nationally. For example, right around a university town it is often hard to find an elementary or high-school teaching position. Many of the students who graduate in education want to remain in the town, so the local school system always has a good supply of applicants. However, if a student is willing to move, job opportunities are likely to be excellent.

Socioeconomic factors. Most students do not like to think that social class, race, or gender have any bearing on career decisions or career opportunities. A significant part of the American ideal is the belief that career mobility is tied to educational attainment and competence, not to the social-class structure. Laws prohibit employment discrimination on the basis of race, religion, gender, ethnicity, and age. However, it is worth pointing out that the laws would not be needed if discrimination problems did not exist.

The impact of socioeconomic background variables on

career decision making can be both subtle and obvious. Subtle influences have to do with the student's own perceptions about which fields are open and desirable. For example, career opportunities in pharmacy are excellent, yet few minority students elect that field of study. Similarly, even though many women are now enrolling in colleges of business, few choose to study finance, and there are few women faculty in the field. As students make decisions, they are indirectly influenced by the absence of role models with whom they can identify.

Among the more obvious influences of socioeconomic variables on career decision making is the cost of a career. Medicine, for example, is a costly field. Students have to anticipate four or five years of medical school after the bachelor's degree. Many medical students complete their schooling with fifty or sixty thousand dollars or more of debt. They then have to work as residents for several years before they can be licensed. They may be thirty years old before they are able to function as a fully independent practitioner. Medicine is only one example of a career that requires a substantial financial commitment beyond college.

Students from low-income families may feel that they simply cannot select careers in which they have to delay their earning power beyond college. They may be unwilling to risk such large personal debts when they have so few financial resources to fall back on. They may not know how much debt their potential earning power can support.

It is important to advise your child to examine the alternatives for financial support carefully before rejecting any career path. Often, sources of financial aid can help reduce the costs of education. What is more, students should be encouraged to weigh the financial costs against the potential satisfaction of pursuing a field that is the best match for their talents and interests.

Psychosocial and emotional factors. Career decisions are influenced by aspects of an individual's personality. The process of pursuing a course of study brings students into contact with particular demands, conflicts, and challenges. Students need to find a good match between the strengths of their personalities and the demands of their fields. Of course, careers and personality types do not correspond exactly. However, some careers place higher priority on certain personal characteristics and less priority on others.

For example, some fields, like surgery, sports, the performing arts, and certain areas of business, require a person to perform at a high level of competence under pressure. If students have a great fear of failure, or if they have trouble making decisions quickly, they will probably not be drawn to these fields. Some students who have considered professions in these areas discover that they cannot perform well and look for related careers that do not require this ability.

As another example, some fields, like accounting, chemistry, and library science, place a high value on very systematic, careful analysis of information. They require a slow, careful, patient approach to problem solving. Students who are impatient and who like to reach decisions quickly probably will reject these fields and go into other areas.

A combination of experiences during the college years contributes to the formation of a commitment to a career goal. As students become more fully enmeshed in their majors, they have experiences that more closely resemble actual work life. They may work for a professor on a project, assist in a laboratory experiment, take a summer job in a related area, have a supervised internship or field placement, or participate in a volunteer program related to their interests. Usually these hands-on experiences contribute to the sense of commitment and interest in the field. Students think about and visualize their work life in the future. Sometimes the experiences help students realize that they are not well suited for the actual work life in a field they were considering.

Students begin to apply concepts they learned in class to real problems. They begin to appreciate the dynamic nature of their field by recognizing those problems that do not quite fit the textbook model. At the same time, they become interested in pursuing certain questions in greater detail as they appreciate how much more information they need in order to address the real work situations they encounter.

The interaction between the principles and ideas learned in class and the problems faced in the field creates the energy that sustains further inquiry. As students become aware that their field is evolving, they may identify opportunities where they can make a contribution. Career decisions take focus as students discover a satisfying fit between their own abilities and interests and an aspect of work where their efforts can be valued.

ADDITIONAL READING

Bolles, R. N. (1990). *The 1990 What color is your parachute?* Berkeley, CA: Ten Speed Press.

Holland, J. (1985). *Making vocational choices: A theory of careers.* Englewood Cliffs, NJ: Prentice-Hall.

Osher, B. and Campbell, S. H. (1987). *The blue-chip graduate: A four year college plan for career success.* Atlanta, GA: Peachtree Publishers.

Personal and Social Problems

*T*his chapter is meant to enlighten, not frighten. We will present a wide range of personal and social problems that occur on college campuses and that are being discussed on campuses today. Probably many of the problems are also present in any community. However, this may be the first time college students have had to confront them on their own. Even if your son or daughter does not have any of these problems personally, he or she may encounter them in a friend, a roommate, or a sorority or fraternity member. Students may find themselves in a position of having to take care of someone who is experiencing a serious problem or to try to find help for that person.

Through conversations, you may find that your child is troubled by what he or she is observing or hearing. You may be asked for your advice or help. With this in mind, the chapter gives you a brief introduction to some of the more common troubling problems students face.

Most college campuses are structured in a way that places a high value on autonomy. Therefore, they usually tolerate a wide range of acceptable behaviors. Students may act in unusual ways, ways that would not be considered appropriate in your family, community, or workplace. Yet other students are reluctant to tell them they have gone beyond the limits. In addition, the typical transitions of the period from eighteen to twenty-two often bring with them patterns of behavior that are unusual. Many of the antics that characterize college life are considered part of the experimentation and personal exploration that is expected during these years. Periods of moodiness, withdrawal, excessive behavior, or overt rebelliousness may all be considered normal for college-age youth. Sometimes students are in the midst of acute identity crises in which they are experiencing high levels of uncertainty or rapid transformations in self-definition. At these times, students may feel as if they are crazy.

Colleges and universities anticipate that many students will need psychological support. Colleges hire staff who can provide different types of guidance and support. Residence hall advisors, financial aid counselors, academic advisors, advisors to student organizations, coaches, and faculty all have different types of professional training that allow them to assist students or to refer students to the appropriate professional for help. Most colleges have counseling centers where the staff is trained to recognize the common social and emotional problems that students confront. They are familiar with the wide range of difficulties that students are likely to encounter in the significant transition from childhood to adulthood. They are able to distinguish problems that are a result of the developmental transition from problems that may be more serious and long-lasting. Usually these services are offered free or at a minimal cost.

Colleges also have various outreach programs to make

contact with students who might not seek out counseling. Programming through offices of women's services, minority student services, gay and lesbian services, disability services, career counseling and placement, as well as through the student union, the residence halls, and student organizations is likely to address critical social and emotional issues. These include suicide prevention programs, rape prevention education, drug and alcohol awareness workshops, crisis hotlines, and AIDS education. In addition, most colleges offer support groups and workshops to help students cope with special aspects of personal identity formation and mental health such as stress management, assertiveness, and communication. There may be support groups for homosexual students, single-parent students, minority students, students whose parents are experiencing divorce, and many others.

Even with all the resources available, parents remain a very important source of support, information, and advice. By maintaining open communication, you can get a sense of how your children are coping with the demands of college life and their own emerging identities. You can evaluate how well your children are handling the conflicts and challenges associated with their emerging independence. When they or one of their friends has a problem, you can help put the problem in perspective. You can give them your view of just how serious this problem is, what resources might be available to help them cope with the problem, and how to seek out the resources.

Sometimes parents conclude that their children are not confronting a problem that really is serious. This is more difficult. If people do not experience any pain, they are not likely to seek help. Generally it is not effective to insist that a person seek help if that person does not think anything is wrong. Therefore, if you think your children are having problems that they do not recognize, you may have to emphasize that their behavior is having a negative impact on someone they care about—you, other family members, their friends, or someone they love. You may also point out how this problem may prevent them from achieving some other life goals. These two approaches may be successful in helping motivate them to cope more effectively with the problem or to seek help if necessary.

DEPRESSION

Depression refers to feelings of sadness, a loss of hope, a sense of being overwhelmed by the demands of the world, and general feelings of discouragement. Most everyone experiences depression at some time or another. You may refer to it as the "blues," being "down in the dumps," or feeling "low." People who suffer from depression experience symptoms including worrying, moodiness, crying, loss of appetite, difficulty sleeping, tiredness, loss of interest or enjoyment in activities, and difficulty in concentrating. Depression can range from mild, short-lived periods of feeling blue to severe feelings of guilt and worthlessness, withdrawal from any social contact, and thoughts of suicide.

College students are likely to experience depression. The feelings can result from a number of causes. Students often come to college with high expectations for success. They are among the top students in their high schools, students in whom others have placed a great deal of hope and pride. College reorders all those people who had strong high school records. Some students discover that in comparison to others at college they no longer come out on top. This may be true in academics, in athletics, in popularity, or in leadership. Thus, some students begin to doubt their worth in relation to their college peers.

Students encounter a very heavy work load in college. They may find that within a few weeks they have fallen behind. In order to cope with the work, they may stay up late, give up their social activities, or do a less thorough job on their studies than meets their standards. Even with all these efforts, they may not be able to catch up. Their academic coping strategies just do not work. All these experiences—feeling overwhelmed, being tired, feeling socially isolated, feeling helpless, and not performing in line with personal standards—can contribute to feelings of depression.

Students who go away to college also give up their social support system from home. They leave family, relatives, and friends who care about them. Most freshmen become homesick or depressed from time to time. It usually takes five or six months to begin to feel that a new social support system is taking shape in the college environment. Especially for students who are not accustomed to college, whose parents never attended college, or who are members of a racial or ethnic minority on campus, feelings of social isolation may result in depression.

As part of the identity formation process, students undergo natural periods of self-examination and questioning. Basic assumptions about personal values and goals, gender roles, career plans, political values, and personal characteristics are reexamined. This questioning is associated with increased feelings of doubt about life's meaning. In addition, academic course work in philosophy, ethics, religion, and literature can raise many of these same questions about the purpose and meaning of human life. This personal inquiry can stimulate feelings ranging from mild depression to despair.

In addition to the factors that can produce depression, many college students are unfamiliar with depression itself. They have not had many experiences with crises, loss, or other events that have produced strong feelings of depression; so they have not developed strategies for reducing these feelings. They may not be able to redefine the situation or focus their attention on some activity that will help them regain their positive outlook. They may have trouble laughing, telling jokes or seeking out humor. Because they feel worthless, they do not seek out others, and they become increasingly isolated. As a result, their depression may intensify.

Other students learn to cope with depression. They seek out others to talk with who will encourage them when they are depressed. They engage in positive experiences that provide feelings of competence to balance their feelings of incompetence. They are motivated to build new skills or take on new challenges to overcome feelings of helplessness. They have favorite music, poetry, movies, or athletic activities that they know will cheer them up. They learn to redefine a situation so it does not seem so bad. They learn to seek out laughter. They understand that their depressing feelings will pass, and they do not let themselves get too far into them.

Treatment for depression depends on its intensity. Many students learn to cope effectively with periods of depression with the assistance of parents, counselors, advisors, intimate companions, and supportive friends. Feelings of depression become a signal that it is time to take a fresh look at the situation and reexamine one's goals, priorities, and commitments. Students who have mild forms of depression can also benefit from short-term counseling. Students who have more severe and prolonged symptoms of depression should definitely seek a thorough psychological evaluation and follow the treatment plan suggested by professionals.

SUICIDE

About 1 percent of all deaths in the United States each year results from suicide. Although the rate of suicide is highest among the elderly, the rate among young people in their late teens and early twenties has steadily increased. Suicide is the third most common cause of death in this age range, after accidents and homicide.

Suicide is usually associated with feelings of being overwhelmed by a problem. In that sense it is closely linked to depression. For students, the problem may be feelings of shame associated with failure to meet a standard of excellence, loss of a love relationship, or social isolation. Usually the young person who commits suicide is at the end of a long chain of problems in which there is a growing sense of alienation from loved ones, or feelings of failure and worthlessness. The young person becomes convinced that the situation is hopeless. Rather than trying to seek help through psychotherapy, the student comes to the conclusion that the only solution is death.

The belief that people who talk about suicide will not actually harm themselves is not true. Whenever people talk about killing or harming themselves, it should be taken very seriously. This kind of conversation is evidence that suicide is being considered, and a person who has these thoughts should be strongly encouraged to seek psychotherapy.

Among college students, suicide attempts far outnumber actual suicides. Although males are more likely to actually kill themselves, females are more likely to attempt suicide. Suicide attempts are associated with feelings of depression, often linked to the recent death of a loved one, a serious argument or break up of a love relationship, or another serious loss. Suicide attempts are often associated with alcohol or drug abuse. The person may be ashamed of the addiction and feel helpless to overcome it. Among adolescents, the rate of suicide attempts is difficult to ascertain since many accidents, especially single-car automobile accidents, are thought to be suicide attempts.

Attempted suicide is usually viewed as a cry for help. The person typically feels cut off from other forms of supportive communication. The suicide attempt is a desperate way to bring the person's despair to the attention of others. About 20 to 30 percent of those who attempt suicide will try again. Thus, psychotherapy and social support are very critical forms of intervention.

Suicide, although an uncommon occurrence in any population, is extremely troubling to those who know the suicide victim. College students who know a student who has committed suicide or who has attempted suicide may experience a variety of emotions, including guilt over not having been able to help the person, anger and frustration about the person's refusal to seek help, and grief over the loss of a friend. For many students, this will be the first encounter with the death of a peer—a sudden realization that life can come to a close. Some students may idealize the suicide victim, seeing the decision as heroic. They may consider suicide themselves and may need treatment.

Whatever your child's reaction, you need to be able to accept and reassure your child that strong feelings are a part of this crisis for the survivors. What is more, you need to help your child understand that suicide is not a real solution to problems of failure or loss. Each human life is filled with problems. It is the courage with which we acknowledge and attempt to overcome these problems that brings dignity to life. Young people must believe that others understand the struggles they are confronting and will accept them when they fail as well as when they succeed.

ALCOHOL AND DRUG ABUSE

Alcohol and drug abuse are probably the most common forms of serious behavior problems observed during the college years. We all have times when we really don't want to cope with life's challenges. We might like to close our eyes to our responsibilities or look to someone else to take care of our problems for us. Many people use alcohol and other drugs to put the worries of their day behind them, to drift into a mellower state of mind. However, we know that for college students to continue to develop, they have to learn to confront and cope with these challenges. Whether the problems are academic, social, athletic, or problems of self-understanding, they need to be tackled in an active, direct way. Floating around in a mist of drug-induced intoxication waiting for problems to go away will not work.

Alcohol is the most widely used and most widely abused drug among college students. Alcohol is a part of the college culture. Binge drinking—heavy and continuous drinking over a two- or three-day period—is considered by some college students to be an acceptable part of having fun. In some campus subcultures, binge drinking is viewed as a special rite of passage for males, a sign of their masculinity. Students do not consider binge drinking dangerous, nor do they think they have a drinking problem if they drink in this way. They believe that this type of drinking proves that they have control over their alcohol consumption. They think they can start and stop when they want to.

However, intensive binge drinking can result in accidents, especially automobile accidents, confusion about taking other medication or drugs, and erratic behavior. In some cases, heavy weekend drinking leads to exhaustion that interferes with studying. Extreme overconsumption of alcohol, like any other drug, acts as a poison in the system and can result in loss of consciousness and even death.

Within the college culture, alcohol has a variety of uses. It is part of celebrations, like sports victories and graduation ceremonies. It is part of marking the end of the week, as in Thank God It's Friday (TGIF) parties. It is part of fraternity and sorority social events. The drinking age in most states is now twenty-one. Most colleges and universities are instituting greater restrictions on alcohol use than ever before, but it will be a long time before alcohol use is eliminated from the college culture.

Alcohol is a central nervous system depressant. In small amounts, it increases sociability and helps people relax. That is why people tend to use alcohol when they are trying to meet new people, to lose their inhibitions, and to feel part of the crowd. Alcohol also becomes the college cure for rough times. It is used to combat depression and frustration associated with getting a low grade on an exam, breaking up or having a fight with a romantic partner, feelings associated with parental divorce, or being rejected from graduate or professional school. Ironically, since alcohol is a depressant, moderate to heavy drinking often has the impact of making a person feel even more discouraged rather than lifting the spirits.

With all these culturally acceptable uses of alcohol, it is hard to know when alcohol use is becoming a problem.

Alcohol use is considered problematic when the person becomes dependent on alcohol to make it through daily life. Alcohol dependency may be both physical and psychological.

Alcohol dependency poses a variety of risks. One potential problem is that students may develop a tolerance for alcohol. This means that they have to drink more in order to get the same effect. The physical damage that alcohol causes, especially liver damage, is accelerated as alcohol consumption increases.

A second problem occurs when alcohol consumption results in loss of control, lapses of judgment, or memory lapses during drinking. Young people may get into fights, take risks, or spend money frivolously when they are drunk. Drinking exposes them to people and problems that they then have to deal with when they are sober.

In some cases, students lose control of their drinking. They cannot stop drinking when they want to. They may drink in the morning to get over a hangover from the night before. They may drink alone as well as with friends. They become unable to concentrate on their studies and begin to take an attitude of indifference to the advice of their friends.

Abuse of other drugs has many of the same characteristics as alcohol abuse. However, it has some important differences. First, many of the other drugs that college students use and abuse, such as marijuana, cocaine, LSD, or stimulants, are illegal. Therefore, purchase of those drugs involves additional risks. It may bring students into contact with criminal dealers and pushers. It exposes students to the risk of criminal charges. In terms of future life choices, a criminal record during the college years may close off certain career opportunities. Since the drugs are illegal, their quality is not controlled. The use of illegal drugs brings with it health risks associated with the unpredictable potency, purity, and dosage of the drugs.

A second difference is the addictive nature of many of the drugs, especially heroin, cocaine, codeine, opium, or other drugs derived from them. The physical sensations are intense. Unpleasant withdrawal symptoms follow the "high," which leaves the person seeking another dose in order to relieve the discomfort. Thus, dependence is readily established. Since the drugs are expensive and difficult to obtain, sustaining the drug habit becomes a major focus of attention and effort.

Drugs other than alcohol that are most commonly abused by college students are the stimulants, often used to keep awake and alert during periods of high demand or to assist in weight loss; barbiturates, often used to help reduce anxiety and to overcome sleeplessness; and hallucinogenic drugs, like marijuana, used to alter and intensify sensory experiences.

In all cases, the primary problem is one of determining whether the student is experiencing dependency. Does the student take the drug repeatedly to achieve the desired effects or to prevent the negative effects of withdrawal? Does the consistent use of the drug prevent the student from dealing effectively with the challenges and demands of the college setting? Does the effort and risk involved in maintaining access to the drug interfere with the student's ability to perform academically or to establish satisfying social relationships?

Drug dependency is extremely difficult to treat. The person must see the dependency as a problem and seek treatment before any progress can be made. Many college students do not see their drug use as affecting anyone but themselves. They may deny that their drug use is hurting them and argue that it is no one else's concern since they are not hurting anyone else. There are a wide variety of treatment programs, but none can work without clear motivation on the part of the addicted person. In addition, the person usually has to try to alter the life circumstances that surrounded the addiction. This may mean finding new friends and reducing exposure to certain life stressors. College students who have become addicted may need to leave the college environment temporarily or permanently in order to live a drug-free life.

EATING DISORDERS

Cultural emphasis on slenderness for women plus the intense focus on weight control in certain areas of athletics, gymnastics, and dance result in two related eating disorders: anorexia nervosa and bulimia. Anorexia is the more commonly known disorder and is observed primarily among adolescent and young adult women. Some young men also suffer from the condition. Anorexia is self-starvation linked with excessive fears of being fat. Sufferers of anorexia view themselves as overweight, even when they are very slender. They seem almost afraid of eating and may restrict themselves to starvation-level diets for days. After a while, the resulting malnutrition interferes with their capacity to reason. They stubbornly insist that they are overweight and may begin strenuous exercise and the use of laxatives to promote further weight loss. Their thoughts are preoccupied with food, weight, and physical appearance.

Bulimia is a related condition, also linked to a fear of being overweight. Bulimics indulge in food binges followed by self-induced vomiting. The behavior is compulsive. Bulimics cannot seem to help themselves from overeating or from the subsequent vomiting.

The conditions have been linked to several factors. Most young people with eating disorders appear to need to exercise control over their lives. They often come from families where they had little opportunity to express their own views or to differ from their parents. They have grown accustomed to trying to conform. Through eating disorders, they attempt to conform to the norm of slenderness and to take charge of their bodies by carefully regulating their intake.

Others who have eating disorders have an excessive fear of fatness. It is as if they believe they will be punished if they get fat. For some college students this may be true. Dancers, gymnasts, swimmers, and divers feel strong pressure to maintain a slight body build. In many sports, a lot rests on being able to qualify for a certain weight category. We find students deliberately manipulating their body weight through dieting and/or binging. Students who are on athletic scholarships have much to lose if they cannot control their body weight.

Finally, some suggest that staying thin is a way for young women to fend off the inevitable transition from childhood to womanhood. In fact, one of the consequences of anorexia is absence of the monthly menstrual period. By struggling to keep their childlike body shape, these young women may be desperately trying to hold back the sexual, social, and emotional changes that will come with adult status.

Treatment of eating disorders is very difficult. Anorexics, even more than bulimics, are not troubled by their condition. They do not see their bodies as others do; and they are pleased, not worried, by their weight loss. Expressions of concern from friends or family are perceived as attempts to control their behavior. Treatment usually requires hospitalization involving a combination of psychotherapy and a controlled, carefully monitored program to reshape their eating behavior. Even when a normal body weight has been established, the person is likely to continue to need psychotherapy and is likely to have difficulty maintaining healthy eating patterns.

SERIOUS FORMS OF MENTAL ILLNESS

Some students who have been treated for mental illness during high school are able to come to college. Sometimes these students, still under treatment, experience more severe symptoms as a result of the stresses of independent living and academic life. In other cases, serious forms of mental illness arise for the first time during the college years.

One of the more common and debilitating forms of mental disorder among American youth aged fifteen to twenty-five is schizophrenia. Schizophrenia is a general term for various mental illnesses in which thinking and reasoning, emotions, interpersonal relations, and day-to-day behavior are all affected. Schizophrenics have trouble relating their thoughts and feelings in a logical way. They may become withdrawn, respond in very inappropriate ways, and experience delusions and hallucinations. Delusions are elaborate systems of thought not based on reality. Hallucinations are sensory experiences that do not correspond with reality, such as hearing voices.

Schizophrenics often complain that they have trouble thinking. They may believe that some force is influencing their thoughts, that their thoughts are being transmitted to someone else, or that their thoughts are dangerous—capable of burning a hole in their brains. In some cases, schizophrenics speak in patterns that are unintelligible, putting words together in strings that do not make sense.

The causes of schizophrenia are not fully understood. Some people definitely have a genetic predisposition for the illness, but life factors may also play a part. Stress in a person's life or a sudden loss of social support may reveal a poorly developed and disorganized personality. Sometimes the pressures and expectations for independent living that are associated with college disclose a lack of personality integration in someone who previously had been able to cope acceptably within the structure and support of the family.

The severity of symptoms associated with schizophrenia and other serious mental disorders is frightening. Other students quickly recognize that they cannot be of much help. The person's behavior may deteriorate over a period of five or six months while friends and family members watch helplessly. If your child believes a classmate is experiencing psychotic symptoms, he or she should encourage the person to seek psychological counseling. These are extremely serious problems, not ones that can be helped by friendly conversations in the dorms. However, it should come as no surprise if the person does not agree to get help. The person's ability to reason about the situation may be so disturbed that the person cannot take positive steps on his or her own behalf. If the classmate's behaviors become disruptive or destructive to self or others, you should encourage your child to alert a counselor, a mental health professional, or, in cases of emergency, the campus police.

Once it is diagnosed, schizophrenia can be treated through hospitalization and drug therapy. However, the chances for full recovery are very difficult to predict. Only about 30 percent of those diagnosed as schizophrenics can resume a fully independent life.

SEXUALLY TRANSMITTED DISEASES

Sexually transmitted diseases, also known as venereal diseases, are infections passed primarily during sexual intercourse. These infections are caused by organisms that thrive in dark, warm, moist areas; the human genital tract is a perfect home for the organisms. Once they begin to grow, they can travel to other areas of the body and affect internal organs. Although the initial symptoms of the disease may disappear, the disease itself is not cured; and the infected person can continue to infect others.

Sexually transmitted diseases are acquired more often by people who have many sex partners during a year. During the 1970s, changing attitudes toward sexual permissiveness led to a greater acceptance of sexual activity outside of marriage. The attitudes were reflected in the sexual activity of college-age men and women. By 1980, more than 75 percent of college males and more than 60 percent of college females acknowledged that they had experienced sexual intercourse. The simultaneous increase in the use of the pill as a form of contraception led to new levels of vulnerability to infection, since couples who were sexually active did not use condoms or other contraceptives that would serve as barriers to the transmission of infection. In addition, most young adults were confident that a sexually transmitted disease could be cured readily with antibiotics.

Today college students face new risks associated with sexual activity. Herpes, hepatitis, and AIDS cannot be cured by drugs. AIDS (acquired immune deficiency syndrome), which is a fatal disease, can probably be prevented by taking precautions related to sexual activity. Young people who are sexually active are strongly advised to limit their sexual activity to a small number of partners whose sexual history is known and to avoid unprotected sexual activity. Abstinence is still the best protection against AIDS and other sexually transmitted diseases. Concern about the spread of herpes and AIDS on college campuses has led to more active sex-education programming, greater emphasis on basic concepts of personal hygiene, up-to-date testing programs, and freer access to condoms in student unions and residence halls.

UNWANTED PREGNANCY

About 30 percent of sexually active adolescent and college-age females become pregnant due to the inconsistent use or absence of contraception during sexual activity. In other words, very few of the pregnancies are planned.

Whether a young woman decides on an abortion or chooses to deliver her child, unwanted pregnancy is an emotionally difficult experience. Most college women who get pregnant perceive their pregnancy as a mistake. They may associate this mistake with a failure to exercise independent judgment. They may criticize themselves for being too gullible about the promises their partner has made. At the same time, they may feel that they should demonstrate their independence by dealing with all the consequences of their pregnancy on their own. This is especially likely if they believe that their parents will reject them as a result of their actions.

Early sexual activity is often accompanied by strong feelings of disappointment. In many cases, the momentary feelings of intimacy are not followed by the ability to build an enduring love relationship. No new sense of closeness, no new bonds of caring are established. Some young women look to their unborn child to fill those needs.

College women who become pregnant are in a vulnerable emotional state. They are likely to be depressed and angry. They may withdraw from social interaction, seeing social rejection and the anxiety they have about their pregnancy as necessary punishment for their actions. They may try to deny their pregnancy, thereby delaying prenatal care.

Unwanted pregnancy can also create a crisis for the college male who has fathered the child. Being responsible for an unwanted pregnancy can lead to feelings of guilt and shame. In many instances, the pregnancy leads to a decision to drop out of school in order to help support the child or to marry before completing college.

These students need help in understanding that their situation is difficult but manageable. They need support from friends, family members, health care professionals, and academic advisors to help them consider the alternatives open to them, including abortion, giving their child up for adoption, or raising the child themselves. If they choose to keep the child, they need to find resources that will make it possible to take responsibility for their child and still continue to make progress toward their academic goals. College students who experience unwanted pregnancy need counseling to help them understand their feelings about the pregnancy, their decision about abortion or their new parental role, and their future sexual relationships.

BIGOTRY

Throughout this book, we have emphasized the positive contributions of diversity to college life. College students have the chance to encounter people from very different cultural backgrounds, racial and religious orientations, and life-style preferences. Students' ideas, values, and goals take shape as they encounter other students and teachers who challenge their assumptions and who want different things out of life. Progress on identity formation requires exposure to differences and freedom to explore alternatives.

However, as a by-product of diversity, college students may encounter bigotry. Many students come to college from very narrow, sheltered family and community backgrounds. They believe that they know what is right and best for them. They have strong, negative, stereotyped ideas about certain religious, racial, ethnic, or life-style groups. They may resist pressures from adults on the college campus to learn about other points of view or to open themselves up to new ideas.

One way of resisting pressures to change is to direct hostility toward people who are different. Thus, we find examples of intergroup hostility on college campuses ranging from subtle forms of social rejection to anonymous bathroom graffiti, to overt, bigoted remarks, to open violence between individuals or groups.

It is sad to say that it is not only students who exhibit acts of bigotry. Some faculty, graduate teaching associates, and staff also behave in disrespectful or prejudicial ways toward certain students. These adults may have had very limited experience interacting with students from a particular background. They may believe that students from one or more groups cannot succeed in college or do not belong at their college.

Students may confront hostility directed toward them because they are a member of a religious, racial, cultural, or ethnic group; because of their gender; because of their social class background; because of their sexual orientation; because of their political ideology; or because of the part of the country they come from. Students who have never been confronted with bigotry before are likely to be stunned. Some part of their identity has been slurred. Just as they are trying to come to terms with how the various aspects of their personal and family history are going to play a part in their own vision of the self, they are forced to defend this aspect of their identity and protect themselves from attack.

Other students who may have experienced this kind of hostility before may be deeply disillusioned by its presence on the campus. They may have hoped that the college environment would be a place where people would accept and value differences. The attacks call into question what an academic environment is all about and what value it has for them.

Still others are strengthened in their determination to resist this kind of hostility. They become involved in campus efforts to educate the community and to make sure that overt acts of bigotry are punished.

Students who have been targets of bigotry on campus need to find a safe adult who can listen to what has happened and who can help the student decide on the best course of action. Most campuses have offices of minority affairs, affirmative action, women's services, or other easily identifiable names where staff will help students cope with these problems. Students need to be reassured that hostile actions are not acceptable in the campus community and will not be tolerated. Students who have experienced bigotry may also want to seek counseling to help them deal with the feelings that are aroused in them by the attacks.

CHEATING

Students know about cheating from elementary school, middle school, and high school. This is not a new problem. However, students may feel a new sense of responsibility to report cheating in college or a new sense of personal outrage when cheating takes place. Someone else's cheating may place them at a personal disadvantage. Students who have never cheated may feel new pressures to cheat in college because of the increased costs associated with failure. They may also discover that cheating is treated with a new level of seriousness at college.

Most colleges have a code of student conduct that outlines how cheating is defined and how it will be handled. Since students are involved in quite a lot of independent work, they have many opportunities for collaboration with other students. Students are encouraged to make use of existing written resources, including books, articles, and published reports. Guidelines state clearly how to give credit to a source when preparing a paper. Students are expected to follow the guidelines, making sure that they do not take credit for ideas or written work that was done by someone else. To include statements written by someone else without acknowledging the author is a form of cheating. To buy a term paper or use a friend's term paper as one's own is a form of cheating.

Cheating can also take place during examinations. Students may sneak in notes when no notes are permitted, copy from another student's paper, or sit for an exam for another student. Students have a variety of ingenious strategies that they use to cheat. Students have been known to steal exam questions in advance so they can study them. Students have been found to cheat during an exam by using a headset over which another student was reading information about the exam.

College students have to understand that they cannot wait to become ethical professionals until after they have received their degrees. The temptations to cheat in some form or another only get greater, and the supervision becomes less direct once they are out of college and into the world of work. It is critical to face and overcome those temptations during college.

Students also have to struggle with the moral decision to identify cheating when they know about it. This takes a great deal of courage. Students do not like to make moral judgments about one another. However, in order to create a fair system that gives each student an equal chance to excel, students must take the responsibility to speak out against cheating. Students should inform their instructor immediately when they see cheating taking place or know about dishonest practices being carried out by other students. It is then up to the instructor to evaluate the situation and to take the proper steps to determine the guilt of the students who were involved.

We have touched on a wide variety of problems that students may encounter on college campuses. We want to reassure you that the vast majority of students manage to progress through the college years without having any of these serious problems. At the same time, most students can tell you about others who have struggled with these problems, sometimes with a tragic end. The problems highlight just how challenging the college years can be. No real growth occurs without some risk. No real change occurs without giving up something. To make the transition from childhood to adulthood, students have to let go of some of the comfort and security from the past and accept new levels of responsibility as well as uncertainty.

As parents, we hope we have prepared our children to have the courage to give up what is necessary and to take the necessary risks. But some children are more vulnerable than others. They may not have the underlying personal strength to manage these pressures all alone. They may refuse help. When young people are struggling intensely to demonstrate their independence, they may resist asking for help. They may deny their problems, resent the advice of others, and even withdraw from those who appear to be reaching out to them. When we see this happening, we hope to guide these students toward the resources that can be of greatest help to them. Above all, we must reassure students that it is not a sign of failure to seek help. Rather, seeking help is a sign of courage, an effort to take charge of their destiny.

ADDITIONAL READING

Monte, C. F. (1990). *Merlin: The sorcerer's guide to survival in college.* Belmont, CA: Wadsworth.

Rowh, M. (1989). *Coping with stress in college: Everything students need to know to manage the pressures of college life.* New York: College Entrance Examination Board.

9 | Conclusion

Why do we send our children to college? Most people would probably answer this question by talking about education and economics—taking courses, learning more, becoming an expert, getting ready to begin a career, securing a financial future. Certainly a college education provides access to new information and higher levels of earning. But in this book we have emphasized that the college years are a time to establish a personal identity. These are the years when young people are open to a thorough self-examination. These are the years when they are intellectually complex enough to entertain a wide variety of ideas, values, and goals. College provides both the freedom and the stimulation that allow this creative process to unfold. A college education is a total experience that not only fosters intellectual growth but personal growth as well. It is not possible to separate the influence of the college experience on intellectual development from its influence on personality formation and the development of social relationships.

A SUMMARY OF ADVICE

What follows is a summary of the ideas and suggestions that have appeared in the preceding chapters. These suggestions are offered in the hope that they will provide useful strategies for continuing to build a satisfying relationship with your children during the college years and beyond.

How can we protect our children from serious mistakes and still convey confidence in their ability to make their own decisions? Reflect on the high school years as a basis to evaluate your children's decision-making ability and judgment. To the extent that you have trusted your children in the past and have been proud of their decisions, you should have confidence about their decisions in the future.

Replace your own automatic advice and opinions with invitations for your child to use his or her ideas and to ask for your advice as needed. Encourage your child to make use of various sources of information in reaching a decision. Discuss the consequences and · trade-offs of various alternatives. Involve your child in family decision making.

When college students make decisions that differ from those you would have preferred, try to remember that you and they have overlapping but not identical futures. The choices they are making have to stand them in good stead for their own adult years.

As your child gains independence, so do you. Take some time to examine your priorities and to explore new goals for your own personal development. Achieving personal identity requires creatively integrating interests, talents, and goals within a framework of socially acceptable roles and values. Support college students through periods of uncertainty as they try to identify their talents, interests, and abilities and as they explore a variety of roles and values.

Encourage students' full use of the college or university to explore components of their personal history and ancestry.

Recognize and encourage your child's accomplishments in whatever areas they occur.

Use your insight about adult life to help your child understand the impact of the demands of work, family, and community roles in adulthood.

Don't overreact to your child's experimentation and role playing. View it as a necessary aspect of identity exploration.

Don't be too enthusiastic or too worried about early commitments your child makes—they may not last.

Keep an eye open for evidence that your child is experiencing an intense identity crisis or profound inability to make any commitments. You are in the best position to recognize these problems, having had the chance to observe your child's approach to decision making and problem solving in the past.

Each college has a distinct atmosphere. It is important to be informed adequately about the college, its intellectual and social climate, and its resources before selecting not only the first-choice college, but the second and third.

Visit campus to see for yourself how your student is adjusting. Try to observe directly if he or she feels comfortable or ill at ease. Read all the signals to determine whether your child is coping well with the college environment. Try to evaluate how much conflict he or she is experiencing in the value climate of the college. Is this conflict growth-promoting or disorienting?

Let your child know that you understand that the first few months, even the first year, of college can be rough. Keep the door open to the possibility that he or she will decide to change to another college or leave college for a while.

One cannot overestimate the importance of a supportive friendship group for helping students feel at home and successful at college. Let your children know that you understand and value their friends.

Encourage students to take time to get to know people who are different from them. Conversations, friendships, and cooperative projects with students from various racial, religious, ethnic, and social class backgrounds comprise a valuable component of a fulfilling college education.

Forming romantic relationships is a major area where new learning takes place during the college years. Students discover important aspects of their own personalities while learning how to meet the needs of someone else.

For some students, high school love relationships become destructive. Parents can help their children take an objective view of these relationships, encourage their children to stay on course academically, and gain distance from the situation.

Reassure your child that it is natural to move on to new romantic relationships and that the capacity for caring continues to develop throughout adulthood.

Play your role in a young adult's love relationships cautiously. Children may look for approval from parents about their romantic partners. Don't be overly critical or overly enthusiastic—try to take a stance of courteous neutrality.

Encourage your student to take a long-range outlook on his or her career decisions and to remain focused on the broadest possible view of the value of a college education.

Expect that college students will change majors and career goals two or three times during the first few years of college. This is typical and should not be a source of great concern for parents or children.

Most students have resolved their uncertainty about a major by the end of the sophomore year. They may decide on a career choice then or during their junior or senior years.

If your student is having trouble making decisions, first ask yourself whether he or she is experiencing healthy exploration or a more serious inability to make a critical decision. If your child is stuck, you should try to intervene. Listen carefully to why he or she is having trouble. Determine if the problem lies in some structural problems about the college, the student's lack of confidence, or both. If there are structural problems, encourage the student to talk with an advisor, department chair, career counselor or admissions officer. If the student lacks confidence or clarity, encourage him or her to talk with a career counselor.

Help your student take a realistic look at factors that influence career decisions. Help him or her strike a balance in considering these factors.

Clarify the career expectations you have for your child and release him or her from unrealistic demands.

Understand the phases in the development of values so you can interpret them. Although it may appear that students are less certain about their beliefs and values during their college years than they were when they arrived, some amount of what looks like backsliding is actually very productive.

It is especially difficult for parents to respond to their children during the period when children see all values as relative. Your objections to your child's value statements may result in your child accusing you of being "hung up" on a narrow view. Try to recognize this as a form of experimentation leading to a longer process of establishing enduring commitments.

Parents are an important source of advice and help when children face problems. Maintain open communication to get a sense of how your children are coping with college life. Help them put the problems they are experiencing or hearing about in perspective.

Students can be very troubled by the actual or attempted suicide of one of their college friends or acquaintances. Reassure your children that strong feelings are part of the crisis for survivors when someone commits suicide. Encourage them to talk about their feelings and help them see that suicide is not a real solution to problems of failure or loss.

If your son or daughter knows a classmate whose thoughts and behaviors are seriously disturbed, advise your child to urge that classmate to seek psychotherapy. Your child may need to alert a counselor or mental health professional if the classmate's behavior becomes destructive.

Reassure students that seeking help to solve difficult social, academic, and emotional problems is not a sign of failure but a sign of maturity. It reflects a willingness to explore options and to take responsibility for one's future.

At its very best, college has a profoundly humanizing effect. During the college years, students become more caring, more responsive to the needs of others, more appreciative of the achievements of human culture, more capable of taking a stand for what they believe, and more willing to work hard to reach their goals.

Part of the humanizing effect results from encounters with differences. Whether it is through their course work, their encounters with other students, or their involvement in student organizations, students experience a variety of demands to consider many points of view. The self-centered perspective of the college freshman is gradually replaced by a more flexible outlook. Students learn to suspend their judgments, to look for evidence, and to examine the logic behind different arguments. They come to respect differences as necessary to a rich, intellectual life. Students understand that they need to encounter different points of view in order to recognize and clarify their own perspectives.

Another part of the humanizing effect of college involves the deepening of personal relationships. Through their close friendships, their involvement with staff and faculty mentors, their identification with campus leaders, and in their romantic relationships, students take new risks of self-disclosure. They explore issues of loyalty and betrayal. They learn to rely on others, to give and receive help, to comfort and encourage one another, and to celebrate one another's achievements. They examine their values and explore new roles in the company of friends who understand and accept them and who permit them to be as uncertain and as unpredictable as they need to be.

Exploring ideas contributes to the humanizing effect of the college experience. As students read Plato, study the American Constitution, recite French poetry, and learn Newton's laws of motion, they become entwined in a chain of human inquiry and reasoning. They discover that they have many of the same questions that have been asked by poets, scientists, and philosophers for generations. They experience a great sense of satisfaction as they discover explanations for complex events, the same satisfaction that has been part of the education of generations of students before them. Students learn that they are part of a continuing human search for knowledge and truth.

Finally, the process of exploration that is part of forming a personal identity contributes to the humanizing effect of college. Students who take full advantage of the college environment to try out different roles, to examine a variety of values and ideas, to explore different majors, and to consider a variety of scenarios about the future usually experience a time of painful uncertainty. This is the price of growth. Students go through a time of not knowing, a time when no view of themselves or their future is compelling. This painful time when they feel very alone, very small and overwhelmed, adds to their capacity for compassion. As their personal identity is formed, they retain this new ability to understand the isolation and helplessness of others. They become more accepting of their own frailties and more forgiving of others.

BIBLIOGRAPHY

Astin, A. W. (1977). *Four critical years: Effects of college on beliefs, attitudes, and knowledge.* San Francisco: Jossey-Bass.

Astin, A. W. (1989). *The American freshman: Norms for 1986.* Los Angeles: American Council on Education and University of California at Los Angeles.

Baum, A. and Valins, S. (1977). *Architecture and social behavior: Psychological studies of social density.* Hillsdale, NJ: Lawrence Erlbaum.

Bell, R. R. (1981). *Worlds of friendship.* Beverly Hills, CA: Sage.

Bryn Mawr College Alumni Bulletin (Summer, 1981).

Chronicle of Higher Education, January 14, 1987, "Fact File." pp. 8–9.

Clayman, C. B. (1989). *Encyclopedia of medicine.* New York: Random House.

Cottle, T. J. (1977). *College: Reward and betrayal.* Chicago: University of Chicago Press.

Erikson, E. H. (1959). Identity and the life cycle. *Psychological Issues, 1,* Monograph 1.

———. (1968). *Identity: Youth and crisis.* New York: Norton.

Fischer, J. L. (1981). Transitions in relationship style from adolescence to young adulthood. *Journal of Youth and Adolescence, 10,* 11–23.

Gerst, M. S. and Moos, R. H. (1972). The social ecology of university student residences. *Journal of Educational Psychology, 63,* 513–525.

Goethals, G. W. and Klos, D. S. (1986). *Experiencing youth: First person accounts* (2nd ed.). Lanham, MD: University Press of America.

Josselson, R. (1987). *Finding herself: Pathways to identity development in women.* San Francisco: Jossey-Bass.

Marcia, J. E. (1966). Development and validation of ego identity status. *Journal of Personality and Social Psychology, 3,* 551–558.

Meer, J. (July, 1985). Loneliness. *Psychology Today,* 19, pp. 28–33.

Michaelis, D. (1983). *The best of friends: Profiles of extraordinary friendships.* New York: William Morrow and Co.

Murphy, K. and Welch, F. (1989). Wage premiums for college graduates. *Educational Researcher, May,* 17–26.

Newcomb, T. M. (1962). Student peer group influence. In N. Stanford (Ed.), *The American college* (pp. 469–488). New York: Wiley.

Newman, B. M. and Newman, P. R. (1983). *Understanding adulthood.* New York: Holt, Rinehart and Winston.

———. (1986). *Adolescent development.* Columbus, OH: Merrill.

———. (1991). *Development through life: A psychosocial approach* (5th ed.). Monterey, CA: Brooks/Cole.

Newman, P. R. and Newman, B. M. (1978). Identity formation and the college experience. *Adolescence, 13,* 312–326.

Null, R. L. (1980). University residence hall suites: A progression of approaches to evaluation research. *Housing and Society, 7,* 67–76.

———. (1981). Student perceptions of the social and academic climates of suite living arrangements. *The Journal of College and University Student Housing, 11,* 6–12

O'Neil, J. M., Ohlde, C., Tollefson, N., Barke, C., Piggott, T., and Watts, D. (1980). Factors, correlates, and problem areas affecting decision making of a cross-sectional sample of students. *Journal of Counseling Psychology, 27,* 571–580.

Perry, W. G., Jr. (1968). *Forms of intellectual and ethical development in the college years.* New York: Holt, Rinehart and Winston.

Sullivan, K. and Sullivan, A. (1980). Adolescent-parent separation. *Developmental Psychology, 6,* 93–104.

Tangri, S. S. (1972). Determinants of occupational role innovation among college women. *Journal of Social Issues, 28,* 177–199.

U.S. Bureau of the Census. (1987). *Statistical abstract of the United States: 1988* (108th ed.). Washington, DC: U.S. Government Printing Office.

U.S. Bureau of the Census. (1988). Marital and living arrangements: March, 1987. *Current Population Reports,* ser. P-20, no. 423. Washington, DC: U.S. Government Printing Office.